NEW TOWNS IN-TOWN

NEW TOWNS IN-TOWN

Why a Federal Program Failed

by Martha Derthick

with a Foreword by
Joseph A. Califano, Jr.

THE URBAN INSTITUTE
WASHINGTON, D. C. 1972

ISBN 87766–022–0
Library of Congress Catalogue Card No. 73–187564
UI 94–112–21

Refer to URI–70006 when ordering.

Available from:
Publications Office, The Urban Institute,
2100 M Street, N.W., Washington, D.C. 20037

List price: $2.95

B/74/3M

FOREWORD

THE CONCEPT of the program to build new towns in-town was
founded on what seemed to those of us in the Johnson Administration involved in urban affairs to be two relatively obvious proposi-
tions:

— The first was that cost of land and the time it takes to assemble
large enough blocks of land for the construction of housing constituted the greatest roadblocks and causes of delay in the construction
of low and moderate income housing units. We had increasingly
come to recognize that the skyrocketing costs of construction were
less attributable to increased labor costs than they were to the increased cost of money and the increased cost of land. Moreover, the
need to borrow money for the long periods of time usually consumed
in assembling large tracts of land aggravated the cost of financing the
construction of new communities.

— The second was the delay caused by involvement of local
citizens: their traditional involvement in terms of humane relocation
policies and the revolutionary concept of poor people's participation
in the planning and construction of new housing or new communities. Any method of easing the human displacement problem saved
not only time, but also removed the profound social impact of
relocation—which often had a severely damaging effect on the families involved.

As this book indicates, there was a definitely impulsive aura to the
beginning of the program. Yet, those who have spent large portions
of their lives in urban planning will recognize that the impulse was
sparked by years of frustrated attempts to build sufficient low and
moderate income housing within large cities.

Against this background, Martha Derthick analyzes seven projects,
none of which, as of the time of publication of this book, achieved
more than minimal success, and all of which failed if measured by an

objective of constructing significant amounts of housing and "total communities" in large cities in relatively short periods of time.* The roadblocks to the program almost caricature American life in the 1960s and 1970s: weak mayors, objections from Capitol Hill, racial concerns, clashes between conservationists and urban planners, difficulties in making the federal bureaucracy responsive to presidential initiatives.

Miss Derthick's study provides us with a microscopic look at a relatively small federal program. It is done in the classical political science tradition: there are no villains and no heroes. There is simply detailed and painstaking analysis of the functioning of institutional government from the highest and most centralized level in the White House, through the states, municipalities, and counties to the lowest and most decentralized level of fragmented citizen groups.

For those of us who have tried over the years to crack the tough nut of urban reconstruction, Martha Derthick's book provides vivid examples of how hard the shell is. One of the most remarkable—and indeed disturbing—aspects of her study is that there are no "bad guys." All those involved—the President, mayors, congressmen, local citizens, conservationists, blacks and whites, private and public developers—were trying to make the program work.

Perhaps most importantly, this book provides a micro-study of the macro-problem of the federal system in the 1970s. It is a system of fifty states and 25,000 cities and counties. It is a system where jurisdictional boundaries were first drawn by Pilgrims and frontiersmen and later refined by the political maneuvering of state and local officials, invariably on the basis of considerations utterly irrelevant to America in the 1970s. It is a system whose gears are often rusted as much as they are greased by the introduction of fragmented neighborhood groups and the decline of the two-party system in urban areas.

There are a great many lessons in this book for those who are dealing with the problems of housing and community development

* Now in the hands of private developers, it does appear that the Fort Lincoln project in Washington, D.C., may finally be getting off the ground.

in urban America today, and for those who aspire to solve those problems in the future. True, Martha Derthick provides analysis, not solutions. Yet the examples are so painstakingly reconstructed that I, at least, would welcome another bite at this apple with the background of analysis that her book gives us. Acting with this background provides no guarantee of future success, but it does provide a means of avoiding some of the roadblocks and blunders of the first new towns in-town program.

It is unfortunate that the papers concerning this program, presently resting in the Johnson Library, had not been released while Miss Derthick was doing her research. Those papers might have provided an insight into the frustration of the President, who sensed so well the desperate lack of decent housing and local communities in the center cities and who, even in the federal city of Washington, D.C.—where presumably the White House would have had maximum control—was unable to achieve what must be regarded as a relatively modest goal in terms of our needs as a nation.

It is singularly fitting for The Urban Institute to finance and publish a study of this kind. For this is one of the central reasons for the formation of the Institute. Participants in the drama of the new towns in-town program are institutionally incapable of self-analysis: those of us who worked on this program at the White House, the mayors of Washington and other cities, the conservationists, blacks and whites who objected, the congressman who withdrew his support. Human nature is such that participants instinctively become expert in the art of hindsight self-defense that follows every governmental failure. Moreover, the views of participants are bureaucratically myopic: if conservation were your goal, then you succeeded in San Francisco; if community participation were your goal, then you succeeded in Washington; and if the creation of a new town in-town were your goal, then you failed in those cities.

Thus, it falls upon detached analysts—free from the bias of self-engagement, free from the need to measure success through a narrow prism, and free from the urgency of inaugurating yet another program to help solve the urban community development problem—to review what has gone before. Even if these analysts cannot tell us what should be done in the future, at least they show us clearly what happened in the past.

Martha Derthick's book is history of a highly relevant and contemporary nature. As such, her book should command the attention of those interested in helping make our federal system work better— even in a nation of people who consider themselves virtually immune from the lessons of distant history.

JOSEPH A. CALIFANO, JR.*

Washington, D.C.
March 1972

---

* Mr. Califano was Special Assistant for Domestic Affairs during the Administration of President Lyndon B. Johnson.

CONTENTS

ACKNOWLEDGMENTS

THE RESEARCH for this book was sponsored by The Urban Institute with funds provided by the Department of Housing and Urban Development. Editorial and publication costs were also provided by the Institute from funds from the Ford Foundation. Obviously the opinions expressed are those of the authors and do not necessarily reflect the opinions of The Urban Institute or its sponsors.

I am grateful to William Gorham, President of the Institute, and especially to Morton L. Isler, director of housing studies, who sponsored the project. I would also like to thank Maureen Ring, secretary to Mr. Isler, for frequent and highly competent help.

I owe a heavy debt to John B. Clinton of the U.S. Department of Housing and Urban Development, who permitted the use of the department's files on the new towns in-town program. Except for a few interviews and some peripheral searches in other agencies, the HUD records are the major source for the following analysis.

To make explicit what will be evident throughout this volume, I wish to make the following disclaimer at the outset: The federal government's efforts to build new communities does not end with the new towns in-town program of the Johnson Administration. Other efforts are under way as the result of laws that provide subsidies to new town developers. These laws were enacted in 1968 and 1970, after the new towns in-town program was launched, and this study does not deal at all with the ensuing projects.

MARTHA DERTHICK

But there is another way as well, which we should encourage and support. It is the new community, freshly planned and built.

These can truly be the communities of tomorrow—constructed either at the edge of the city or farther out. We have already seen their birth. Here in the nation's capital, on surplus land once owned by the Government, a new community is springing up.

President Johnson's Message on Housing and Cities to the 90th Congress
February 26, 1968

The trouble with the White House—for anyone who is a part of it—is that when he picks up a telephone and tells people to do something, they usually [agree to] do it. . . . the heel click at the other end of the wire will be audible and the response . . . will be prompt. There will be no delay in assurance, however protracted may be performance.

George Reedy
The Twilight of the Presidency
1970

INTRODUCTION

ONE RESULT of the social activism of the 1960s was that Americans grew disillusioned with government. As criticism of social conditions rose, so did the level of government activity; but regardless of how much government had achieved in the way of social improvement, it had led the public to expect more. The more government tried to do, the plainer became its inability to do very much, or at least all that its leaders said it would. Both the right and the left attacked it for failing to fulfill its promises. This charge was made especially against the federal government; among the many governments in this country, it is obviously the largest and the one most conspicuously committed to social improvement.

If the federal government is unable to do in domestic affairs what its leaders say it will, this is not necessarily because the men who run it, either as elected officials, presidential appointees, or high-ranking civil servants, are lazy, incompetent, or deceitful. If they delude the public as to what to expect of government, it is because they delude themselves as well. They too are puzzled and disillusioned when things go wrong and government programs do not fulfill their promise. In my experience, they welcome attempts by scholars to explain why things go wrong; they too want the answers. They want them even more eagerly than the rest of us, for their pride and satisfaction in their work are at stake.

Why, then, do federal officials make promises they cannot fulfill? Or, assuming the flaw is in "the system" rather than the men who run it, why is the government so unresponsive to experienced leaders? To help answer these questions, this study examines one case of government failure—an attempt by the Johnson Administration to create model new communities on federally owned land in metropolitan areas. The program began in the summer of 1967. Four years later, no new communities had been built. Practically none had even been started. Thus the program was unequivocally a failure. Not only did it fall short of its goals; it produced few visible results of any kind.

The program seemed promising when President Johnson launched it. The President had high hopes for it, and it was hailed by various organizations with an interest in community development, including the U. S. Conference of Mayors, the National Housing Conference, the American Institute of Planners, and the National Association of Housing and Redevelopment Officials. In addition to the development aids the federal government was already offering to local governments—grants for planning, urban renewal, and housing construction—it would now make available the resource of land. This combination seemed likely to produce results.

In part the program failed because the federal administration's search for sites did not yield many. Though the federal government owns a vast amount of land, most of it turned out to be in the wrong places or the wrong size for developing new communities in urban areas. What was suitable for development was not necessarily surplus; federal agencies were using it, or expected to. Sometimes, even where sites were available, local officials had no interest in developing them. In only seven places were conditions so promising that the Johnson Administration announced plans to carry out projects.

Even in these seven, however, the program failed. Three projects —in San Antonio, New Bedford, and San Francisco—died outright. The other four—in Washington, Atlanta, Louisville, and Clinton Township, Michigan—encountered serious difficulty and delay; as of the spring of 1971, fewer than 300 units of housing were actually under construction. Whether any project would be completed—or, if completed, would fulfill the federal administrators' conception of a model new community—was uncertain.

This book describes what happened to each of the seven projects and analyzes why the program failed.[1] The conclusions of course are

1. Because events have been reconstructed from HUD's files, the narrative reflects the perspective of federal officials. The author is responsible, of course, for the use made of those files and for the analysis. The Urban Institute asked qualified readers from each of the seven cities to review the cases for accuracy, but otherwise local sources were not consulted except in the District of Columbia.

circumscribed by the framework within which the cases occurred. The new towns in-town program fitted a particular institutional pattern, that of an attempt by the federal government to act in cooperation with local governments, and it was directed toward a particular type of objective, community development. As an analysis of why federal government programs fall short of their promise, this case yields one set of answers rather than a comprehensive answer that is generally applicable.

Even as a federal attempt to assist local governments with community development, the new towns in-town program is unusual, for it was solely a presidential program. Congress did not take, and was not asked by the Administration to take, any action regarding it. Its origin was unusual, and so was its fate. Few federal government programs fail as thoroughly as this one did.[2]

By examining an extreme case of failure, this study should reveal something also about success. Even among the seven projects of the new towns in-town program, some failed faster and more thoroughly than others. By comparing these cases, and by briefly comparing the program as a whole to other federal programs, one sees not just why the federal government failed in a particular case, but what the conditions of success are likely to be.

In general the program failed because of disabilities of the federal government associated with, and to a degree inherent in, its central character. Very simply, the program was an unsuccessful attempt at centralized action in a governmental system that remained extremely decentralized more than a generation after the New Deal and two decades after World War II.

---

2. And few disappear even if they fail. As of the spring of 1971, the new towns in-town program retained a tenuous existence as a responsibility of the Office of New Communities in the Department of Housing and Urban Development. One civil servant was assigned part-time to follow through on old projects and look for possible sites of new activity.

I · THE PROGRAM

1 ORIGIN AND OBJECTIVES

THE PROGRAM was President Johnson's idea. One morning in August 1967, as he was sitting in his bedroom at the White House and talking to Special Assistant Joseph A. Califano, Jr., it occurred to the President that federally owned land in the cities could be used for housing. Within hours, his staff had assembled a working group from the executive departments to figure out how this could be done.

Housing for the poor had been much on the President's mind. No public need seemed more urgent. Riots spreading through the nation's cities seemed to be the slum-dwellers' protest against the conditions of the slum. To build new housing was one way to improve those conditions. Furthermore, no need had so exposed the limited ability of American governments to act effectively. Construction of new housing for the poor in the central cities had practically come to a halt. The President and his staff had been casting about for months for a way to overcome this problem. They were concerned first with the substance of it—they wanted to improve the living conditions of the urban poor. And they were concerned with its symbolic significance—they wanted to act in order to prove that effective action was possible. By supplying a critical resource—land —the President hoped to increase housing construction in a dramatic way.

The federal government was already trying to produce good

housing for the poor. Since 1937 it had provided cash subsidies to local public authorities for constructing public housing to be rented to persons with incomes below a specified level. Since 1961 it had been providing mortgage insurance at below-market interest rates to certain private developers. This program, known as 221(d)(3), was designed to produce homes for "moderate-income" persons—those who were not poor enough to qualify for public housing yet were too poor to afford decent housing that was unsubsidized. Through the urban renewal program, the federal government supplied a variety of subsidies for clearing and rebuilding city land. This program could be used (though in practice it rarely had been) to help produce new housing for the poor.

The President believed that if another kind of assistance and another affirmation of the federal will were added to these, the problem might be overcome, especially if the additional aid was land. If the federal government could make the land available cheaply, as the President assumed, it would reduce one major economic obstacle to construction. It would also very much reduce the political and administrative obstacles that often thwarted housing projects at the local level. No one—at least no one whose protest need carry much weight in local politics—would have to be relocated. The usual process of assembly and clearance would be vastly simplified.

The program also appealed to the President and his staff because it would not require new legislation. Laws providing for disposition of federal surplus land, along with the various housing and development laws, would provide the statutory underpinning; the surplus lands program would get results by exploiting what had already been enacted. To men who wanted results in a hurry, this was an exciting prospect.

The President wanted to start the new program in the District of Columbia. As the federal government's own city, it would be relatively responsive to his initiative. Action there would be highly visible and thus effective as a demonstration to other cities and to members of Congress of what could be done. And a splendid site was already available—335 wooded, rolling acres in the northeast corner of the city that had been occupied by the National Training School for Boys. Because the school was moving to West Virginia, the land would soon be ready for redevelopment.

Had this attractive site just a few miles from the White House not existed, the President might not have conceived of the surplus lands program at all. "We wanted to do it all over the country," one of his assistants later said. "We wanted to do it well in Washington first so that every mayor and congressman could see it could be done."

The Planning Session

It was the end of the workweek when the President had his idea, but his staff nevertheless called a meeting right away of high-ranking officials from the agencies concerned—the General Services Administration, the Department of Housing and Urban Development, the Department of Justice, the Bureau of the Budget, and several agencies of the District government. The immediate objective was to get the pilot project started in the District. The rest of the program could wait until it was launched.

Though the men who met at the President's call were under pressure to make decisions in a hurry, they were by no means unprepared. For more than two years, since it became known that the training school site would be available, several local and federal agencies had been laying the groundwork for redevelopment with informal and intermittent negotiations. Both the National Capital Planning Commission (NCPC) and the D. C. Redevelopment Land Agency (RLA) had explored various methods of housing development, RLA with the hope of using an urban renewal project at the fringe of the city to facilitate relocation of residents from projects at the core. But it was clear, an RLA official later recalled, that "if this thing were going to go, you'd need some head-knocking." When the President himself knocked heads, the thing went very fast indeed.

The group convened by the White House produced a plan in three days. It proposed to the President a "balanced residential community" of 4,000 to 5,000 housing units. Everyone at the meeting agreed that to develop the whole site with housing for the poor would be a social disaster. Instead the government should plan for a mixture of social classes, yet the mixture proposed heavily favored the less well-off and thus preserved the President's purpose. From 1,200 to 1,500 units were to be public housing and another 1,800 to 2,200 would be 221(d)(3) housing. Only 800 units would be conventionally financed and thereby restricted to the better-off.

The planning session concentrated on two problems. One was whether redevelopment could be subsidized with federal urban renewal funds. Because the land was unoccupied except for a few training school buildings, it could not qualify as a blighted urban area. It could qualify as an "open land" project, but this would entitle the District only to loans, not grants, and without grants the District government might have difficulty getting enough money directly from Congress to finance the project. District redevelopment officials had hoped for a third possibility—that the site might qualify as a "predominantly open land" project, which, like a conventional project, would be eligible for grants.[1] However, following an inspection of the site early in 1966, HUD regional officials had found that it was ineligible. Now HUD changed its mind. Walking the site on a Sunday morning with the President awaiting a response, HUD officials from Washington headquarters decided that the site *could* qualify as a predominantly open land project. The other question had to do with land disposition. By law, GSA had to sell land at fair market value, but if the training school site were to be developed with low-income housing, as the President and local agencies wished, it would have to be sold for less than that. The planning session yielded no definite statement of how this problem would be solved, but officials from HUD and the District redevelopment agency, at least, understood that GSA would lower its asking price to a point that would make construction of low-income housing feasible.

In a summary of the meeting for the President, GSA Administra-

1. Under federal urban renewal law, a project may consist of land in any of three categories: (1) "a slum area or a deteriorated or deteriorating area"; (2) "land which is predominantly open and which . . . substantially impairs or arrests the sound growth of the community"; (3) "open land necessary for sound community growth which is to be developed for predominantly residential uses." Federal assistance for an "open land" urban renewal project should not be confused with that for acquisition of "open space." The former is meant to promote development; the latter, to preclude it.

tor Lawson B. Knott, Jr., assured him that all the federal and local agencies were "in substantial accord concerning the total plan" and agreed "that it is legally and economically possible of accomplishment under existing authority." Enclosed with the memorandum was a schedule of agency actions through November 15, 1968, when the D. C. government and HUD would approve the finished plan. The action plan said nothing about cities other than Washington, but Knott assured the President that what was to be done in the District could be done elsewhere.

With these assurances in hand, the President announced the program to the public on August 30, 1967. He declared that the training school site would become "a new, attractive, and well-balanced community" with "modern housing and services for about 25,000 citizens." Although the announcement concentrated on the District of Columbia, the President made clear that this was the beginning of a national program. He was setting up a cabinet-level task force to survey surplus federal properties in other metropolitan areas and "to evaluate the prospects for transforming these lands into vital and useful community resources."

The President's announcement came less than a week after his conversation with Califano. As a creature of the chief executive, this program was to be invested with the executive virtues—energy, speed, and flexibility.

The Task Force

The program was presidential also in that it was the responsibility of no single department, but depended on the ability of the White House to coordinate several executive agencies. The President began by setting up an inter-agency task force.

The chairman was the head of the General Services Administration, the agency that manages federal property and disposes of surplus land. After the President had his idea about using land for housing, the first thing his staff did was to call Administrator Knott, who played a leading role in the weekend planning session. In a note to the President, Califano praised his cooperation. Both GSA's official role and Knott's own performance made him a logical choice to be chairman. Another obvious choice for membership was the secretary of Housing and Urban Development, Robert C. Weaver, whose department would have to play an important part in helping local governments to develop the land. The Secretary of Defense was added because his department was by far the biggest owner of federal property and thus would have to cooperate in the search for disposable sites. The fourth and final member was the Attorney General, named so that his department could work out legal problems. To achieve the President's purpose it would be necessary to transfer the land cheaply, and to devise a legal strategy for this the White House preferred to rely on the Justice Department's lawyers—young, progressive, high-ranking recent graduates of the nation's best law schools—rather than on, say, the lawyers in HUD, who were more likely to be career civil servants of advanced age ("New Deal types," a White House staff member later said). The White House staff thought that the former could be counted on to make the program work; the latter seemed more likely to frustrate it.

The task force functioned for six months and met half a dozen times, often with alternate members representing HUD, Defense, and Justice. Knott as chairman sent regular progress reports to the President. From the start, the task force had to rely on the departments for administration since it had no staff of its own. It delegated to GSA the principal responsibility for site surveys and to HUD the principal responsibility for planning. It also created a legal subcommittee, an inter-agency group of lawyers headed by a member of the Department of Justice, to study land disposition.

Survey teams entered the field immediately after the President's announcement. During the first week of September they covered seven cities. By the end of October they had covered twenty-six, and by the end of the year, forty-eight, including 509 pieces of federal property. GSA and HUD together assembled the list of metropolitan areas to be surveyed; GSA identified locations of federal land, HUD the locations of housing need. With some exceptions, the forty-eight areas they agreed on were the country's largest. Teams drawn from GSA, HUD, and Defense, with the GSA member as chairman, surveyed each area for sites that the federal government could part with and that would be suitable for housing development. They did not consult local officials.[2]

On the basis of the survey reports, the task force found that sites in twenty-two of the forty-eight areas were suitable. This did not mean, however, that they were actually available. Many had not been declared surplus, and the task force had to initiate that process. In the case of Defense Department properties, this involved clearance with the Armed Services committees of the Congress, which had thirty days to act. To declare the sites surplus invariably involved delay, and in some cases it proved impossible. Military commanders or local chambers of commerce successfully appealed to Congress to oppose release of the land.

When property was definitely available—and in a few cases even before it was—a federal planning team consulted with local officials about prospects for development. Again the team was composed of representatives from GSA, HUD, and Defense, but this time a HUD official—ordinarily the regional administrator—acted as chairman. The planning team described the program's purpose and the President's personal interest in it. It then solicited local cooperation and promised fast processing of grant applications. If local officials agreed to go ahead, the team asked for an "action program" that would outline the locality's plans for development and administrative organization. HUD supplied guidelines and offered the help of regional officials in preparation of such a program. After the local government had submitted an action program and HUD had approved it, the administration announced the project.

Planning team visits were delayed in some cases because HUD wanted to await the outcome of local elections or the reduction of race conflict. Even when visits could be arranged, they did not always evoke local interest. Local officials doubted the need for more housing, thought the federal land better suited for other purposes, did not want to assume the administrative and financial burden of so

---

2. The task force provided also for a second survey method that did involve local officials. Federal officials would begin by explaining the federal government's purpose to local officials and asking them to identify federal property and explain their city's housing needs. This method was used only in New York.

large an undertaking, or were preoccupied with other urban development programs, especially model cities. The few projects that the Johnson Administration announced were those that both evoked local interest and survived the several federal reviews.

Surveys stopped at the end of 1967, but HUD continued to conduct planning insofar as local interest and the availability of land permitted. The task force continued to function until early March 1968, when its chairman recommended to the President that it be dissolved and that HUD take charge. HUD's role had grown as planning proceeded.

HUD's Role

HUD officials were ambivalent about the President's new program.

On one hand, it came without warning from above, a burden imposed by an impulsive, demanding President. It was an implied criticism of their department, born of the President's dissatisfaction with the results of HUD programs. And it came at a difficult time. HUD had been formed as a department only two years before and was still waiting to move into its own headquarters.

Yet the program was an opportunity too. Because it had the President's backing, HUD could benefit from the cooperation of other executive departments—specifically, from their contributions of land. Because it did not depend on legislative action, administrators would be free to prepare their own guidelines and to pick locations for development. They would not have to put a project somewhere to satisfy a committee chairman. Assuming the availability of federal land, they could pick places where the local officials were known to be progressive and to have the capacity for getting things done. Hoping to exploit these advantages, HUD officials soon came to regard the program as a way of demonstrating the newest ideas in city planning and the newest techniques in development. In their hands it became a model-communities program. The more they thought of it this way, the better they liked it.

Interest in new communities had been rising among American city planners in the 1960s, and HUD had been trying to get a federal program under way. Congress had rejected proposals in 1964 and 1965, but minor legislation—a qualified offer of federal mortgage insurance to new-town developers—passed in 1966. HUD officials thought that the surplus lands program might complement this legislation; in any case, it would help HUD to experiment with new communities in urban settings. That the program was confined to metropolitan areas of course meant that it could not be used to build new towns in the strict sense, as relatively large, independent cities apart from existing concentrations of population. But HUD's conception of new towns or new communities (officials used the term interchangeably) was broad and vague, and readily linked to development of the surplus lands.

Within HUD the program was at first assigned to Robert E. McCabe, deputy assistant secretary for renewal assistance in the Renewal and Housing Assistance Administration. Because he was responsible for allocating urban renewal funds and because the availability of such funds was a critical issue in the planning of the pilot project, McCabe was among those whom the White House had summoned to the initial planning session. Secretary Weaver subsequently named him HUD's manager for the program; as such, he arranged planning team visits and drafted guidance for the planning teams.

It was McCabe who first outlined HUD's own objectives. As he listed them for Secretary Weaver on September 11, 1967, they were:

(1) Increase the supply of low- and moderate-income housing in cities with urgent needs. (2) Build a "community" that will foster economic and racial integration. (3) Rapid production. (4) Promote experimentation—new materials, new forms, new systems, new public facilities, and new land use controls. (5) High standards of public facilities. (6) Better and multiple use of public land. (7) Development of a community integrated with, and complementary to, the larger community in which it is to be located.

One of HUD's first acts was to assemble a consulting team to help spell out these objectives in a set of development standards for local governments. McCabe and Undersecretary Robert C. Wood chose members to represent various professions or sectors of activity (engineer, planner, public official, industry, education). With George Rockrise, Secretary Weaver's special assistant for design, as chairman, and with staff support from a dozen or more high-ranking officials of HUD, the eleven man group met at Silver Spring, Maryland, during the last weekend in September and produced a draft right away.[3] Rockrise then took charge of clearing it within HUD.

HUD completed work on the standards by the end of October but did not issue them until February. Delay occurred because the Justice Department was dissatisfied with the provisions governing racial integration. At task force meetings, Attorney General Ramsey Clark insisted repeatedly and single-mindedly on the importance of achieving integration. HUD agreed to revise the standards to emphasize this goal, but it took more than two months of negotiations between Justice and HUD officials at the working level to reach agreement. HUD feared that to accept the strong language sought by Justice would make the program unfeasible almost everywhere in the country. HUD's action-program guidelines for local agencies similarly had to be revised to meet the Justice Department's objections. Prepared in early November, they were not issued formally until April. However, both the development standards and the action-program guidelines were circulated informally while HUD's differences with the Justice Department were being resolved. Thus they were available as guides to those local governments that began projects early.

The development standards declared that "a key objective" of the

3. In addition to Rockrise the members were Fred T. Aschman, an urban planner from Chicago; William Conklin, an architect from New York; Franklin Edwards, a professor of sociology at Howard University; Lawrence Livingston, Jr., an urban planner from San Francisco; Harvey Perloff, an economist with Resources for the Future; David Rowlands, president of the International City Management Association; John Rubel, vice president of Litton Industries; Robert Simon, developer of Reston, Virginia; and Walter Mylecraine and Charles Smith, officials of the U. S. Office of Education. Perloff was the author of an article (*Journal of the American Institute of Planners*, June 1966) from the title of which HUD officials may have borrowed the term "new towns in-town," but not the concept attached to the term. The article proposed rejuvenation of developed urban areas rather than new development. Although conceived by HUD as a way of producing "model communities," the new towns in-town program should not be confused with the model cities program, which Congress enacted in 1966. Model cities is meant to rehabilitate developed areas through larger and better-planned federal expenditures than are possible under categorical grant programs. Among HUD programs, it is more nearly analogous to Perloff's proposal than was new towns in-town.

program was "the creation of an urban community"—a "community of diversity, offering a wide variety of opportunity to a cross section of people with different social and economic backgrounds." The community "should offer opportunity to all racial groups," and should house at least three different income groups—"middle income," "upwardly mobile and potentially upwardly mobile employed persons with low and moderate incomes," and "the 'economic bottom,' including 'hard core' unemployed." This was not meant, however, to exclude the rich. Though all income levels were to be included, distinctions among them in housing design were to be avoided. The model community should *appear to be* integrated as well as *be* integrated. Above all, there should be no recognizable "housing projects."

To attract and retain diverse income and racial groups, it would be necessary to provide "magnets" and to "imbue the residents with a personal interest in the new community." HUD suggested various ways of doing this, principally by providing jobs and high-quality public services, of which education would be most important. "The schools . . . must be the best. That is how disadvantaged groups will be served, and how the better-off, more mobile groups will be attracted and retained." HUD also suggested that a sense of commitment to the community might be fostered by giving priority in residence to the workers who built the community, by experimenting with "various and imaginative forms of homeownership," and by efforts to engage residents in community "action." If local governments would do these things, HUD assured them, they would "help meet the present urban crisis. . . ."

In polishing the draft, HUD eliminated or rendered euphemistic some provisions that local officials would have found provocative. For example, the initial but not the final draft called for minimizing "reliance upon the car, especially the second car," and said that "city departments must agree to decentralize . . . to maximize the delivery of services to the New Town community." The essential concepts, however, did not change as the draft evolved.

In general, HUD officials who reviewed the draft did not seriously challenge it. An exception was Abner Silverman of the Housing

Assistance Administration, who pointed out in a memorandum to Rockrise that HUD's goals were not fully consistent with the President's and asked how they were to be achieved without strong financial incentives. "In one sense," Silverman wrote, "the report suggests that each of these new areas be given a 'model city' treatment without providing the financial incentives inherent in that program."

There was no doubt within HUD that the program would depend heavily on local interest and initiative. At a staff meeting in late October (one of the regular meetings that brought together two dozen or more of the department's top officials), following an explanation of the program by McCabe, "there was general agreement," the minutes say, "that the Federal responsibility is to smooth the way for the local development, crank up the machinery, and turn the project over to the local officials to execute as they determine to be best for the community." There was little consideration, however, of just what would be required to evoke local action or what to do if HUD's guidelines did not square with the local officials' conception of what was "best."

White House staff members[4] at least, if not the President himself (that is not clear), were fully aware that HUD was embellishing the President's objectives, but they did not perceive any conflict. HUD's plans did call for substantial amounts of housing for the poor; if they provided too for amenity, open space, class and racial integration—in short, the elements of a "good" environment—so much the better. White House staff members were confident that the President would not want to be responsible for building new "ghettos." The idea of new towns had independent appeal at the White House too. In August 1967, only a few days before the surplus lands program was launched, Califano had set up an interdepartmental task force on new towns with instructions to prepare "a strong and imaginative program" for the next session of Congress.

As HUD worked on objectives, it also set up an administrative office for the program. To head it Weaver and Wood chose Richard L. Steiner, who had been urban renewal commissioner in the Eisen-

4. Califano and three assistants—Lawrence Levinson, Frederick M. Bohen, and Matthew Nimitz—handled the program at the White House.

hower Administration and later housing development director in Baltimore. His appointment took effect in mid-October. To work with him, HUD detailed a high-ranking civil servant, John B. Clinton, who had been assistant director of the Model Cities Administration. The office soon grew to four professional and two clerical persons. For a while it received policy guidance from McCabe, but under an agreement reached in February 1968, Steiner reported directly to the secretary and undersecretary on policy and to McCabe on administrative matters. In fact, the office had no formal charter within HUD until the end of the Johnson Administration, and lines of authority remained unclear.

As HUD shaped the program to its own purposes and developed its own administration, it acquired a stake in the success of the President's idea. Slowly this presidential program became also a departmental program; along the way, HUD met a number of problems.

One was a continuing confusion over objectives, probably inevitable in a program that had been launched with so little planning. One sign of it was difficulty with nomenclature. Soon after Steiner took charge of administration, he discovered that no one had decided what the program should be called. HUD was calling it "new towns in-town," but Steiner perceptively observed to Secretary Weaver that this title would probably overdramatize the program and encourage expectations that the results would not justify. After reviewing the President's press release of August 30, he recommended that the name be "federal land for critical urban needs" (FELCUN). Though HUD adopted this, the more ambitious conception of model new communities continued to enjoy currency within the department until experience deflated it.[5]

---

5. Formally, the name FELCUN survived until the fall of 1968, but it proved too long and awkward to use. In HUD the program was more often called "new towns in-town," "new communities," or "mini-cities." Steiner then recommended to Secretary Weaver the name "surplus lands for community development" (SLCD) which was used thereafter. In a half-whimsical memorandum, Steiner offered the choice of eleven other names as well: NNEL, New Neighborhoods on Excess Land; NNDP, New Neighborhood Demonstration Program; IN, Innovative Neighborhoods; LAND, Land Available for Neighborhood Development; NNCP, New Neighborhood Construction Program; NCSL, New Communities on Surplus Land; TNT,

It soon became clear that the program would not satisfy either the President's original purpose—to build quickly a large amount of new housing for the poor—or HUD's purpose—to create relatively large, semi-autonomous model urban developments within metropolitan areas. In addition to all the other problems it was encountering, such as lack of local interest and the resistance of military commanders to parting with land, there simply were not enough large sites in the right places to do either of these things. Periodically, therefore, HUD had to explain to the White House staff why it was not making more progress toward the President's objectives, and it had to ask itself anew whether it could make progress toward its own.

A second problem was defining relations with other federal executive agencies. HUD needed to establish control over the program yet retain the cooperation of the other agencies on the task force. From the Defense Department it wanted prompt release of land. From GSA it wanted a selling price for land of less than fair market value. From the Justice Department it wanted indifference rather than repeated intervention in the matter of racial integration. Not only did the Justice Department want HUD's guidelines to set strict standards for integration; it also wanted to participate directly in site selection and planning.

For HUD to establish dominance over the program proved relatively easy. In the conflict with the Justice Department, which occurred before the task force was dissolved, Chairman Knott decided in HUD's favor, declaring that it alone had responsibility for reviewing local plans. The Defense Department had never shown any dis-

---

Tomorrow's Neighborhoods Today; NCIT, New Communities in Town; HOMES, Housing on Metropolitan Excess Sites; HELP, Housing on Excess Land Programs; NEIGHBORHOODS, The Never Ending Interest of the Government in Having Better Organized Recreation, Housing, and Other Objectives on Diversified Sites.

"New towns in-town" is used in the title of this study because it conveys the purpose of the program briefly and with reasonable accuracy. "Surplus lands" is often used in the text because it is briefer still, and having gotten into the text the reader will understand what it means. Because the program's objectives were unstable and ill-defined, it may be preferable to describe the program by reference to the means it employed (surplus land) rather then by the ends it sought (new towns in-town, or whatever).

position to run the program. And GSA, which had borne a large share of the initial responsibility, eventually withdrew voluntarily, with Knott as task force chairman choosing to hand the program over to HUD. For HUD to retain the cooperation of these agencies was of course much harder. As they lost interest in influencing the program, they also became less willing to bear the costs of contributing to its success.

A third problem was internal conflict. The program could create difficulties of resource allocation for HUD's operating units—the Renewal Assistance Administration, Housing Assistance Administration, Federal Housing Administration—and it could put a heavy administrative burden on the regional offices. If the program were to succeed, officials at the top of the department and in the surplus lands project office needed the cooperation of these agencies.

The program threatened to increase the demand from local governments for HUD's funds, especially in the urban renewal, public housing, and 221(d)(3) programs, but at least in the short run it did nothing to increase the supply. (In the longer run, the White House assumed, the very success of the program would increase the supply; Congress would appropriate more funds if the executive branch demonstrated an ability to get results.) Unless operating agencies were willing to allocate funds to surplus lands projects—funds that they might already have allocated in other ways—the program would not succeed. Officials at several points in HUD would have to choose between supporting the President's new program and spending funds in customary ways.

This was a problem, especially for the Renewal Assistance Administration, upon which local requests for subsidies would fall first and perhaps most heavily. In addition, RAA bore the administrative costs of the surplus lands program within HUD. Within RAA it was a problem especially for McCabe. Having been given a share of responsibility for the surplus lands program, he wished to make it a success; but as the administrator of the urban renewal program, he wished to conserve its funds. In preparing guidance for the surplus lands program, he stipulated that preference should be given to "open land" sites—ones that could not qualify for urban renewal grants. He resisted giving renewal grants for local acquisition of the surplus lands, preferring that GSA subsidize redevelopment by reducing its asking price for the land. In March 1968, when HUD acquired full responsibility for the program and Steiner requested an increase in staff from six to thirteen, McCabe argued against raising the level above seven. The extra positions would have deprived other, presumably permanent, components of RAA. (Undersecretary Wood authorized eight positions and promised to review the staffing level again.)

Administrators of the surplus lands program sought assurance from the secretary and undersecretary that their projects would have priority in the allocation of funds and the processing of documents, and to a degree they succeeded. However, statements from HUD's top officials on the priority question were not as firm, clear, or frequent as they might have been, and in any case priorities are established only through usage. If surplus lands administrators were to claim priority successfully, they had first to push their projects to the point of development. Before then they could make no claims for funds at all.

To HUD's regional offices, the program came as a surprise, just as it had to headquarters. Regional officials learned of it when urgent phone calls from Washington instructed them to join survey teams in a search for federal property. (One member of the New York office was ordered to Buffalo on a Sunday morning to look at a large piece of federal property—a shallow stretch of Buffalo harbor, as it turned out.) Sometimes, ahead of the phone calls, headquarters officials came to the regions themselves; the first survey teams were assembled in Washington in such haste that they did not include regional officials. The first planning team, which visited San Antonio on October 5, was staffed from Washington. Not until mid-November did headquarters officials assemble the regional administrators for a personal briefing. In the meantime the regions learned of the surplus lands program from memoranda and random visits of central-office personnel.

This beginning antagonized some regional officials. One regional administrator, Francis D. Fisher in Chicago, objected outright to the program. Fisher argued that officials in Washington had given too little thought to it and that the federal government ought not to tell local governments how to use the surplus land. They should be permitted to pursue the "highest and best use" even if this turned out to be something other than a new community. "If Central Park were a military base," he wrote Secretary Weaver, "it would qualify . . . , yet would a new town in-town be the highest use?" Even after a two-hour meeting in early October with officials from headquarters, who pointed out that HUD's standards would permit a variety of development, Fisher seemed unconvinced.

As time passed, regional officials were given a larger role and more regular guidance, but the central office continued to regard this as a program in which it would play a larger part than usual. ("Good diplomacy," Wood noted on an ingratiating letter that Steiner sent to Fisher in November, "but the [Regional Administrators] should know that this program is run by headquarters.") The animosity of regional officials subsided too. In the longer run, the danger in the regional offices was indifference.

A fourth problem—really a potential problem to which HUD in fact gave little attention—was relations with Congress. If Congress had participated in creating the program, presumably HUD would have been more careful to inform it about administration; but the White House had decided to avoid Congress at the outset, and HUD stuck by that decision. Whether congressmen were to be notified of planning team visits was left to the discretion of GSA, and whether they were to be notified before projects were announced was left to the discretion of the White House. As a rule, they were not notified. HUD re-examined this policy (a policy initially of the task force) in early February, at a time when the project in San Antonio was meeting opposition from a member of Congress, but Secretary Weaver thought that the policy should not be changed. To notify congressmen of projects well in advance would be more damaging to the program, in his judgment, than not to notify them at all, or to do so at the last moment before the public announcement. There was danger of arousing opposition to the program, and HUD assumed that congressmen would not be interested in it anyway unless it meant grants for their districts. From start to finish, surplus lands was an *executive* program.

It was also an intergovernmental program, and if it were to succeed, there had to be at the local level a strong will to make it succeed. Sensing that local opposition could jeopardize the program, Steiner early proposed that planning teams urge mayors to create an "advocate force," a citizens' committee that could combat local opposition. He feared that otherwise opposition would be carried to Congress —specifically in the many cases that required release of Defense Department land, to the Armed Services Committees, where HUD and GSA would have little influence. For the program to work, however, would require more than the combatting of local opponents by local supporters. More fundamentally, HUD would have to induce local support.

The program rested on the assumption that large, vacant tracts of land at low prices would be very powerful inducements, but as time passed the federal government's ability to offer such inducements seemed more and more problematic. Large, vacant tracts in the cities were not numerous, and there were legal obstacles to low prices. The task force report on land disposition, which the legal subcommittee submitted in December, did not support the original premise of the White House that the surplus land could be given away or sold cheaply. On the other hand, it did not flatly deny it. The laws governing disposition were complex and the prospects for exploiting them could vary from project to project. HUD therefore retained hope that the program could work. Forwarding the task force report to regional administrators, Steiner wrote that "the matter of 'fair market value' may be troublesome in some cases, but we must proceed with the program on the assumption that ways will be found through appraisal techniques or otherwise to make land available to ultimate users at prices which make feasible program objectives for low and moderate rent housing."

At the federal level—and, as a consequence, at the local level too— progress depended on the continuing interest of the President. The White House had assumed that a burst of presidential energy could galvanize the federal bureaucracies, and HUD hoped that the energy would be felt still farther away. Whether addressing mayors, its own regional officials, or other federal agencies, HUD headquarters sought to exploit the President's sponsorship. For this tactic to work at all, fresh affirmations of presidential interest would be required. The White House staff and to some extent the President himself did maintain an interest in the program; to the end of the Johnson Administration, HUD officials sensed heavy pressure to produce results. The White House continued to insist on weekly progress reports. But of course the President's interest waned when it became clear that there would not be much progress to report. "He got educated over the fall that this thing wasn't going to go like hot cakes," according to an assistant. Accordingly, the value of presidential sponsorship began to decline, and what remained by the end of March was lost when the President announced that he would not run again. HUD then was left with responsibility for a presidential program that had lost its president.

Origins and Outcome

It might be argued that the origins of the program account for its unsuccessful outcome. In contrast to most federal programs, it depended solely on presidential action; Congress enacted no authorization and made no appropriations. Even as a presidential program it was highly personal; and the President who created it left office sixteen months later, having announced well in advance that he would do so. As a personal creation of the President, it was improvised and hasty. Only one weekend of staff work preceded the announcement, and then the press release constituted the sole documentary foundation of the program. There was no executive order, not even a memorandum from the White House to the departments. These factors by themselves might seem to explain the failure of the program, but they do not explain it satisfactorily.

Though Congress was not asked to authorize the specific program, strictly speaking it was not without a foundation in law. It was founded on many laws. The idea was that it would exploit, through executive coordination, a whole series of existing statutes, and even in retrospect it is not clear that such an assumption was mistaken in principle. Bypassing Congress might also have been a mistake in that Congress alone can provide money, without which no program can succeed. But the program did not fail for lack of money. Few projects reached the point at which they required major expenditure.

The President's leaving office cannot explain the failure, for the program began to fail even before he left, and before he announced that he was going to leave. Had it gone as well as the White House expected, the next administration would have had little choice but to carry it out, at least to the extent of completing projects under way.

And even if it is correct to say that the program failed because it was improvised, that explanation is superficial. It is still necessary to ask what was faulty about the improvised arrangements.

II · THE PROJECTS

2 WASHINGTON

Angry Citizens and an Ambitious Plan

The President today requested Secretary Weaver, Administrator Lawson Knott of the General Services Administration, and Walter Tobriner, Chairman of the District of Columbia Board of Commissioners, to "move at once to develop a new community within the Washington city limits."

The new development will be built on the 335-acre site in Northeast Washington formerly occupied by the National Training School for Boys. . . .

"This spacious open tract," the President said, "can become a new, attractive, and well-balanced community at a major gateway to the Nation's Capital. It can provide comfortable and urgently needed housing. . . . But it should be more than a housing project. Washington needs and deserves the best in community planning—and this new development can be the best of communities."

White House News Release, August 30, 1967

THE PRESIDENT wanted to get off to a fast start in the District of Columbia.[1] This would give the program momentum and show a skeptical public that the government really meant to act. The symbolic purpose of the program—to act for action's sake—had a high priority at the White House, and in any case suited the President's nature. Once seized with an idea for improving his country, he was not a patient man. Effort in the District of Columbia therefore took two forms—constructing "Project One," to consist of 400 housing units on a twenty-acre parcel; and planning the "Fort Lincoln New

---

1. For a more detailed description of this case, see Martha Derthick, "Defeat at Fort Lincoln," *The Public Interest*, Summer 1970, pp. 3–39.

25

Town," the complex new community, named for a Civil War fort, that would occupy the full site.

Both undertakings came as a test for the District's new government—a mayor-commissioner and nine-man city council—which the President had proposed to Congress early in 1967 to replace a board of three commissioners. That the city government was undergoing reorganization might have been a serious disadvantage except that the reorganization itself was meant to increase the local capacity for action. The White House expected that one executive would be more effective than three. And it expected that the new government, as a creature of the President, would be more responsive to the federal executive branch than the old, which was more the creature of Congress. In the new government as in the old, the President would appoint the leading local officials.

The action plan that federal and local officials prepared for the President called for construction of Project One to begin July 1, 1968, to be completed a year later; the first tenants would move in by May 1, 1969. This project would consist of 250 units of public housing for the elderly and large families, and 120 to 150 units of 221(d)(3) housing. Planning for the rest of the development would be done by June 30, 1968; construction would take five to seven years.

Getting Started with Project One

Project One soon ran into opposition from neighboring residents, most of whom were middle-class blacks. If the training school site were to be redeveloped at all, they preferred a use that would secure the middle-class character of their neighborhood. In 1965–66 they had objected to a proposal for building a Government Printing Office plant at the site. Now they objected to public housing. In early October 1967, a group of them protested Project One at a public hearing of the District commissioners. Kenneth Kennedy, chairman of the Northeast Neighborhood Planning Council, demanded that the hearing be postponed until the new city government could conduct it, and then led a walkout.

Local officials responded to opposition with offers of "participation." These offers, however, were not simply a response to citizen action. Thomas Appleby, the executive director of RLA, the urban renewal agency for the District, wanted to achieve citizen participation.

Appleby had frequently affirmed a commitment to citizen participation since coming to the District from New Haven in 1965. As proof of this commitment, in the spring of 1967 RLA agreed to give the Model Inner City Community Organization (MICCO), founded by a black minister and civil rights leader, $200,000 a year to help plan the Shaw urban renewal project in the center of the city. Before neighborhood opposition to Project One arose, but knowing that it was likely, Appleby sought to arrange participation in planning for Fort Lincoln. Among other things, he suggested to other local officials that Kennedy be notified "of all our proposals and plans, inasmuch as he appears to be the leading spokesman in the neighborhood." The appearance of opposition and Kennedy's walkout did not deter Appleby.

After the new mayor, Walter Washington, took office, he too strongly supported citizen participation. The new government, whose sponsors thought of it as a compromise step toward home rule for the District, was generally expected to be more sensitive than its predecessor to citizen opinion, black opinion especially. Mayor Washington and a majority of the council were blacks. Late in November, when the mayor announced receipt of a large ($887,000) survey and planning grant from HUD, he promised "maximum citizen involvement in all phases" of Fort Lincoln's development. At the mayor's invitation, Kennedy sat beside him as he made the announcement.

With this encouragement, Kennedy submitted to local officials a request for funds for the Model Outer City Community Organization (MOCCO), which he had founded as a counterpart to MICCO. Early in December he began to negotiate a contract with local renewal and planning officials. However, before they could reach agreement, RLA got a letter from the president of a community association in the northeast, Jesse Jackson, denying that MOCCO existed and challenging Kennedy's right to speak for the neighborhood. Jackson promptly formed his own imitation of MICCO and submitted a prospectus to RLA. A dispute over citizen participation in the project was beginning to overshadow citizen opposition to it. Confronted with this new claimant, RLA declined to give a contract to either. It told Kennedy and Jackson that they must resolve their differences. Before long a third citizen group, led by white and black clergymen, arose in the northeast to mediate between them, but when that effort failed, it too applied to RLA for funds and recognition.

By the end of February, then, RLA was confronted with three claimants where in November there had been only one. They were unable to settle their differences independently, and Kennedy—who was bitter at the government's failure to recognize him after its initial encouragement—grew hostile and threatening. "You have not kept faith," he wrote Appleby in early February. "The RLA does not wish to involve citizens." And again, two weeks later, "Your inaction compels us to no longer request, but to demand meaningful participation."

Both the dispute over citizen participation, which was highly visible and much publicized, and the initial problem of citizen opposition, which was still latent, could hamper the public agencies' work on Project One. For reasons having nothing to do with local politics, however, work was not advancing fast.

At HUD's urging, Appleby in January agreed to use Project One to demonstrate new housing technology. To HUD officials, Project One was the pilot development in the pilot project for a nationwide model communities program. As such it should serve the objective of innovation. Appleby divided the project into three parcels and assigned each to an architect chosen for his work with a new technology. The three were Moshe Safdie, Paul Rudolph, and Harry Weese; respectively, they were working with concrete boxes, mobile home cores, and concrete panels. RLA signed contracts with them in March.

Innovation—HUD's dominant objective—conflicted with speed, which had been the President's. The architects soon encountered problems with building code specifications, and Deputy Mayor Thomas W. Fletcher decided to set up a task force to study changes in the code. It was late May. Construction could not possibly start in July, as the President had been told. Technical and political problems would have to be resolved first.

Planning the New Town

In January RLA hired Edward J. Logue to take charge of planning the new community. As development administrator in New Haven and Boston, Logue had built a national reputation as an urban expert and man of action. Having recently lost a campaign for mayor of Boston, he was available for the Fort Lincoln project.

As principal development consultant, he was to oversee the work of other specialized consultants (for planning and design, engineering, transportation, etc.); prepare a statement of objectives; set up an advisory panel to help define objectives; review plans for Project One; and prepare a report, in preliminary and final versions, that would cover all aspects of the plan for Fort Lincoln. He would be paid $295,000, of which approximately $235,000 would be for subcontracts to other consultants.

Within the government, responsibility for planning was lodged in a staff committee consisting of the executive director of the National Capital Planning Commission (Charles H. Conrad) as chairman; the deputy mayor of the District (Fletcher); the executive director of RLA (Appleby); and the deputy assistant secretary for renewal assistance of HUD (McCabe), who was added to the committee at HUD's request. Logue was to receive guidance from this committee and report to it. He also had HUD's development standards for guidance.

Logue believed, as did the authors of HUD's development standards, that race and class integration should be the overriding goal. By mid-April, he concluded that this goal could not be achieved with the housing mix described in the President's announcement (1,500 public housing units, 2,200 units of 221(d)(3) housing, and 800 conventionally financed units). The proportion of the poor, nearly all of whom would be blacks, was too high. It would not be possible to draw middle-income whites to the community; over the long run, middle-income blacks might not stay. The staff committee agreed, but was reluctant to change figures that the President had announced. Only after soliciting Secretary Weaver's approval did it tell Logue he could change the housing mix.

Logue also feared that Project One would jeopardize the entire Fort Lincoln community. With 250 low-income units and 150 moderate-income units, it would contain a disproportion of the poor and give Fort Lincoln an unfavorable reputation. Thus Logue sided with neighborhood residents who wanted to delay construction of Project One, and he also sided with them in asking the local government to build a new school at the same time it built family housing. The advisory panel of experts that Logue set up, most of whom were middle-class blacks, became a sounding board for the neighborhood's complaints about Project One. The panel's report, submitted in June, asked that it be cancelled as a separate project.

Again, the staff committee agreed with the substance of Logue's analysis. Officials in both HUD and RLA feared that Project One would kill any chance of achieving the model balanced community. But again they feared to change a commitment to the President, whose desire for a fast start had produced Project One.

In June the secretary and undersecretary of HUD and the District's mayor and deputy mayor considered how to meet the objections to the project yet keep their promise of prompt action to the White House. They decided that all of Project One might be deferred except for some public housing for the elderly, which would be less offensive to the neighborhood and less damaging to the reputation of Fort Lincoln than would family housing, and would not add a single pupil to the schools. They agreed that work on the housing for the elderly should start at the earliest possible moment in order to achieve a groundbreaking before November. They also agreed to build community facilities, especially schools, as promptly as housing.

In mid-July, Logue submitted a report to the staff committee that outlined objectives and a preliminary plan for the entire project. In keeping with HUD's guidance to the staff committee, he limited low-income units to twenty percent of the total. He recommended a mix of 900 low-income units, half of which would be for elderly; 2,250 moderate-income units; and 1,350 middle-income units.

Meanwhile, local officials had acted to settle the dispute over citizen participation, which had troubled Logue's planning effort as well as Project One. After repeated pleas for action from Appleby, Mayor Washington in early June set up the Citizens' Planning Council for the Fort Lincoln Project, composed of fifteen residents of the northeast (five from each of the three rival groups) and eight city-wide members. Henceforth, public officials hoped, planning could proceed with the cooperation of this organization.

In Pursuit of Action

Progress depended on achieving satisfactory designs for Project One, but in late summer, RLA and HUD officials appraised the work of the three architects with discouraging results.

Safdie's design was not feasible and had to be abandoned. Rudolph's design was not feasible either, though it came near enough to justify more work. The principal problem in both cases was cost. The District government was prepared to make building code revisions to accommodate the new technology, but the costs of the technology, at least as applied on the limited scale that Project One permitted, would not come within HUD's limits for public and 221(d)(3) housing. Of the three preliminary designs, only Weese's was feasible.

In addition to this, citizen participation problems recurred. Local officials had hoped that by bringing the rival neighborhood groups together in one organization, they would put an end to delay. This assumed that the new organization would cooperate with the government. In fact the council was extremely hostile. The eight city-wide members, who were meant by the mayor to be a moderating and disinterested force, soon tired of the meetings and left them to the neighborhood members. These members, though still plagued by differences of interest, nevertheless had one opinion in common: that RLA had unfairly excluded them from a share in planning.

Before it would consider plans, the council wished to define its power and secure funds. Early in July it delivered to Appleby a list of seventeen demands that in essence called on RLA to surrender the planning function to it. Having been invited by local officials to submit a budget request, the council at the end of July asked for $820,000, virtually the entire amount of HUD's survey and planning grant to RLA. And in September, it sued the District government and RLA, asking a federal district court to enjoin planning for Fort Lincoln until local officials permitted "meaningful" citizen participation and developed "adequate plans . . . to protect residents in the affected area."

A groundbreaking before November, which Undersecretary Wood had decreed in June, seemed impossible. As of September there were no finished architects' drawings and only one set was in prospect. The government had created a vehicle for citizen participation, but the citizens had gone to court in an attempt to halt planning altogether. This situation precipitated another round of official decision making.

The White House was determined to have a groundbreaking. The President and his staff continued to want action for action's sake. Beyond that, both the White House and HUD wished to get far enough along with the new community that another administration could not turn back. After a meeting on September 20 with Califano, Wood set November 25 as the date for a groundbreaking. Construction was to start with 120 units of high-rise public housing for the elderly designed by Weese. To Appleby's relief, Califano had vetoed a tentative suggestion from HUD to transplant finished designs from an urban renewal project elsewhere in the country.

To get the project ready for construction by November would require the public agencies to make extraordinary effort and hard choices. Within HUD, for example, the Housing Assistance Administration had to give approval hastily, on the basis of incomplete plans and uncertain cost estimates. It balked, not wanting to risk "adverse audit findings," but went ahead after eliciting an explicit memorandum of justification from Undersecretary Wood.

The bureaucrats proved willing to bend their rules, but the mayor was unwilling to ignore the citizens' council. He would not go ahead until it had approved Project One, and it was unwilling even to consider the subject. When, on October 14, it finally did begin consideration, it objected that Project One contained too much public housing. By the end of October it was clear that there would be no groundbreaking by December 7 (the latest choice for a date), and maybe none before President Johnson left office. Clinton wrote Wood on October 30 that "unless the Mayor is instructed by next week to proceed with or without the citizens, this Administration will not have a groundbreaking ceremony."

HUD and the White House pressed the mayor to act. HUD drafted a letter threatening to withdraw funds from Fort Lincoln, and although the letter was not sent, its message reached city hall. Simultaneously, the citizens' council for the first time was showing signs of cooperation. In mid-November it sent Appleby comments on Project One that at least laid a basis for negotiation. The council asked, for example, that the government limit public housing construction to the 120 units for the elderly and that it promise in writing that a new school would be finished before any family housing.

The council had changed its position in response to a change of opinion in the neighborhood, which in turn resulted from the public agencies' offer to build a new school there. In July the District government had decided that it would build a permanent school right away rather than the demountable classrooms to which the neighborhood and Logue had objected. As of early October the House Appropriations Committee had approved funds and local officials were looking for an architect. In this situation, for the citizens' council to obstruct Project One was to deprive the neighborhood of a benefit to which it attached a very high value.

It was still necessary to get the council to go along with the groundbreaking. To do this, local officials agreed to build a school before family housing, and they reduced to twenty-five the number of low-income family housing units planned for Project One—which was twenty-five more than the council wished, but, as Appleby told its president, "the minimum we think is necessary to fulfill our public responsibility." They also sought to reach agreement on the council's funding, which had been at issue since July.

In response to the council's request for $820,000, Appleby had offered $36,500 for a one-year period. In mid-November he raised this to $60,000. The council, which had reduced its request to $316,000, thereupon appealed to the mayor, who doubled Appleby's offer. For its part, the council acquiesced in a start on construction. Because RLA could not or would not spend as much as Mayor Washington had offered, he had to appeal to HUD for the money. HUD found the funds—a grant of $60,000 for a six-month period— in its Office of Urban Research and Technology, which administers urban renewal demonstration grants. Fort Lincoln, HUD decided, would be an appropriate place in which to "demonstrate" the citizen participation process.

The groundbreaking finally occurred on January 15, less than a week before the inauguration of President Nixon. More even than most groundbreakings, this was merely a symbolic event. The architect had finished drawings only for the foundation, and construction did not actually start until May 5.

The Logue Plan

After the Nixon Administration took office, the burden of initiative shifted to the local agencies. Formerly under federal pressure to act, they now had to solicit federal support. This meant that they had to come to grips with the Logue plan. Presumably, they would use it as the basis for grant applications to HUD.

Fort Lincoln, Logue had told the staff committee in July, "must travel 'first class'." In order to achieve the ambitious goals of class and race integration, it must have "an exceptionally high level of public services" and make use of "new approaches in both planning and development." With approval from the staff committee, Logue had proceeded during the fall to elaborate the more ambitious of two preliminary plans. His strategy ,which was wholly faithful to HUD's guidelines, was to attract a balanced population to Fort Lincoln with the promise of "community," and he sought to assure community through a series of measures that would both differentiate Fort Lincoln from its environment, the rest of the District, and integrate it internally.

Logue finished the plan in December. Federal and local agencies reviewed it in January and February, and by early March RLA's Fort Lincoln project director, Arnold Mays, had distilled the results of the review for the staff committee. In a series of memoranda,

Mays analyzed the problems that had been revealed, some of which seemed very serious.

One problem was economic. To provide a large amount of open space, the plan called for extensive use of structured parking, which would raise the cost of housing development well above what HUD could legally subsidize. Mays concluded that it was "highly unlikely that the plan, as presently proposed, could be developed." The economic dilemma was made worse by the failure of GSA and RLA to agree on a price for the land. In August 1967, when the project was conceived, officials from HUD and RLA had understood that GSA would sell the land for its reuse value, but in the summer of 1968, when RLA began negotiations, GSA asked fair market value. It said then that it had no legal authority to sell at a lower price. According to a GSA official who took part in the initial planning session, HUD had misunderstood what was said—GSA had made no commitment to sell at reuse value.

Another major problem arose from Logue's proposal for transportation. Again in order to obtain open space, he proposed use of a minirail, which would consume less land than a street-and-parking system. But neither the cost nor the technical feasibility of such a system had ever been established. In December HUD and the Department of Transportation had agreed to finance more studies of feasibility, but they and RLA had been unable to agree on how to proceed. Besides, more studies could not answer all of the economic, administrative, and technical questions that needed answering.

A third set of questions concerned the schools. Logue had hired as educational consultant Mario Fantini of the Ford Foundation, who had recently helped lead an effort to decentralize New York City's public schools. Along with Milton Young of the Travelers Research Center, he developed "a design for a new and relevant system of education" that Logue incorporated into his plan. In the spring of 1969 the District Board of Education was preparing to sign a $420,000 contract with the General Learning Corporation of New York to elaborate the plan, but Mays was appalled by the vagueness and vacuity of the contract language ("a rehash of the educational mish-mash that has been discussed for months"), and thought the Fantini-Young report inadequate as guidance. He urged the staff committee to develop its own guidelines for the Fort Lincoln school system after consulting with the Board of Education.

Like other elements of the Logue plan, the proposal for education raised serious questions of feasibility. It called for Fort Lincoln's schools to be administered independently of the rest of the city system. The new-town system would consist of a series of "dispersed but interrelated" general learning centers, which would serve as the "home rooms" and fulfill "general academic functions," and special learning centers, which would "provide specialized instruction in the arts, sciences, and practical arts, with an emphasis on 'real life' experience—relating the school curriculum to actual social and economic enterprises on the site." Since this system would cost more than the conventional system in the rest of the city, it would be contrary to a federal district court decision of 1967 (*Hobson v. Hansen*) that prohibited inequality in per pupil expenditure in the District's public schools.

Because the survey and planning grant from HUD expired on June 30, the staff committee hoped to have a plan ready by then, but the Logue plan posed so many problems that Mays recommended against submitting it to HUD. Instead he urged the staff committee to carry out Fort Lincoln under the newly enacted neighborhood development program (NDP), a course that would—if HUD agreed—enable the District to construct Project One with federal urban renewal funds while continuing to plan the rest of the project. With more time Mays hoped to resolve the problems in the Logue plan. In April, following his recommendation, the NCPC instructed its staff to prepare an NDP plan for submission to HUD.

The local agencies also grappled in the spring with two questions of procedure—how to manage construction of Fort Lincoln, and how to manage the intractable problem of citizen participation, which threatened to make a farce of the whole undertaking.

Logue believed that Fort Lincoln should be developed by a corporation with comprehensive powers, and hired a Washington lawyer to show how this could be done. However, lawyers in the District's public agencies were not convinced. The assistant general counsel of the NCPC wrote that the many contractual and informal agreements required were "legally questionable" and "practically untested"; that there was no legal way to avoid the complex series of approval and review steps involved in a project like Fort Lincoln; that it was doubtful that the corporation could be created without legislation, and legislation would take too much time; and that its financial feasibility had not been demonstrated. The staff committee rejected the development corporation and began in April to explore an alternative—a development agency, to be made up of representatives of existing agencies and endowed by delegation with some of their executive powers and a staff.

After HUD agreed to finance citizen participation with a demonstration grant, RLA opened negotiations with the citizens' council over a contract, but in two months had been unable to reach agreement. One issue was HUD's insistence that the council withdraw its suit against the government. Another was a provision that the hiring of personnel have RLA approval. On April 15 the staff committee decided to cease doing business with the council (it had received a petition from northeast residents, including many of the council members' wives, urging it to do so), and began to consider other ways of consulting citizen opinion. With the backing of the mayor, it decided to hold meetings throughout the city at which plans for Fort Lincoln would be presented to civic organizations.

By May the local agencies were ready to take their case to the Administration. Though a formal NDP application could not be ready before fall, it was none too soon to seek federal support informally.

The Federal Response

The local officials took their plea to the White House and to HUD. In view of the amount and variety of federal support it required, Fort Lincoln was unlikely to survive except as a presidential project. RLA had identified nearly a dozen federal "concerns," matters in which federal agencies must act favorably if Fort Lincoln were to be built. The Departments of Transportation, Interior, and Health, Education, and Welfare were involved, as well as HUD and GSA. In particular, local officials hoped that by getting support from the White

House they could put pressure on HUD, the department with primary concern. It would bear $40.4 million of the $51.65 million in federal expenditures that RLA estimated Fort Lincoln would need.

In May and June, local officials made their case, led by Fletcher and Melvin Mister, Appleby's successor as RLA director. (Appleby left when the administrations changed, but Washington and Fletcher, having been reappointed by President Nixon, remained as mayor and deputy mayor.) They briefed HUD officials late in May and then responded to HUD's questions with two long letters that set forth objectives and cost estimates. In mid-June they briefed Daniel P. Moynihan, director of the newly created Urban Affairs Council and President Nixon's advisor on District affairs.

They found HUD skeptical and resistant. HUD officials doubted, as did local agencies, the feasibility of the Logue plan. They lacked confidence in the local government's capacity to execute so ambitious a project, and the longer the citizen participation dispute persisted, the less confidence they had. (An attempt by the mayor's office in June to explain Fort Lincoln to civic organizations was a "disaster," according to an observer from HUD. Leaders of the citizens' council and other black activists broke up the meeting.) Finally, they objected to the cost. In urban renewal funds alone, the District was asking $36.4 million for Fort Lincoln, three times the capital grant reservation that HUD had made in 1967.

The high cost threatened to distort the new administration's priorities, which called for using urban renewal funds to rebuild riot areas—starting in Washington. The Nixon Administration had been in office scarcely more than a week when the President visited the riot areas with Mayor Washington and announced a large grant. Like the Johnson Administration, it was using the capital as a "demonstration city," a place in which to symbolize a commitment to the cure of urban problems.

When the District's request for funds to rebuild the riot areas, which President Nixon had inspired, was combined with its request for Fort Lincoln, which President Johnson had inspired, the total for Fiscal Year 1970 was more than $134 million. That was nearly a sixth of the urban renewal appropriation of $850 million that HUD expected Congress to provide for the whole country. HUD balked. It sought to avoid commitment to any particular development plan. Especially, it did not want to get committed to the Logue plan, and it tried to forestall action by either local officials or Moynihan's office that would lead to such a commitment. In any case, Moynihan shared HUD's doubts about the District government's administrative capacity. HUD ceased to participate in meetings of the staff committee except as an observer, and it explicitly released local officials from any obligation imposed by the Johnson Administration to go ahead with Project One.

Despite repeated signs of discouragement from HUD, the local agencies continued work on a preliminary plan and an NDP application, a strategy that HUD feared would commit it to the Logue plan or something similar. The NCPC was scheduled to approve a preliminary plan on September 11. On September 30, it got a letter from Undersecretary Richard C. Van Dusen saying that "it would be premature" for HUD to commit funds for Fort Lincoln or encourage a start on development activity. Specifically, it would not grant money for Project One beyond what was needed to finish the 120 units of public housing for the elderly.

HUD had not killed the project. A departmental task force, after several months' review of Fort Lincoln and consideration of various alternatives—including disposition of the land by GSA in the normal way—chose to retain the site for housing. Accordingly, HUD agreed to give the local agencies money for more planning and feasibility studies.

The Future of Fort Lincoln

In the summer of 1970, RLA and HUD agreed to seek a private planner-developer for Fort Lincoln. Unable themselves to resolve the problems of design and finance, they invited a private organization to try, specifying that it must adhere to "the primary objective of . . . a well designed socially, racially, economically, and functionally balanced community."

Following a competition, RLA awarded a contract in November for a feasibility study to the Westinghouse Electric Corporation, in combination with Building Systems International, an industrial housing producer. In effect, Westinghouse was given a license to revise the Logue plan, with a promise of a development contract if its revision satisfied RLA and HUD. Nixon Administration officials in HUD seemed determined to insist on a showing of feasibility, and to avoid a major commitment of public funds until such a showing had been made.

Sooner or later, the Fort Lincoln site will be developed somehow. More than 300 acres of prime land in the nation's capital will not lie vacant forever. But whatever happens there, the Fort Lincoln New Town is not likely to be remembered as an example of "the best in community planning." No doubt, that was what Washington needed and deserved, as President Johnson had said, but it was not what it got.

3 SAN ANTONIO:

A Congressman Objects

The White House today announced plans to transform surplus federal land . . . in . . . San Antonio.

The new San Antonio community will be located on 200 surplus acres at Fort Sam Houston. More than 4,500 citizens, mainly low-income families, will be housed on the site. Job opportunities for the unemployed will be provided through special training programs and a light manufacturing center.

Representatives of the Federal Government worked closely with . . . local officials in developing these plans.

White House News Release, December 12, 1967

THE WHITE HOUSE picked San Antonio for the second surplus lands project. The President wanted a project in Texas, and among large Texas cities, San Antonio was a logical choice because it contained both a large number of the very poor and a large stock of federal land. The President asked the task force for a plan by October 23, for he was to be in Texas then and wanted to make the announcement from San Antonio.

The task force did its best to comply. A survey team visited the city early in September and recommended a tract at Fort Sam Houston, about four miles northeast of the city center. In use only as a pistol range, it would require no clearance and the Defense Department was willing to make it available. Because the nearest residential area, Snake Hill, was a black and Mexican-American slum, localized oppo-

41

sition to housing construction seemed unlikely. A planning team visited San Antonio on October 5 and reported an "excellent" reception from local officials. A task force memorandum had already assured the White House "that San Antonio has a good city government and that HUD can work well with it." The mayor said that city officials were prepared to sit down right away with federal officials to develop "a conceptual package."

With federal help, the city produced an action program by October 17. The only problem was that the land had not actually been declared surplus. By law, such a declaration would have to be cleared with the Armed Services Committees of the House and Senate, a process that normally took a month. GSA and the Defense Department thought that it might be hastened in this case if the President would talk to Representative Mendel Rivers, chairman of the committee in the House, but the White House chose not to do this. Instead, the tract at Fort Sam Houston waited in line and got clearance in the routine way, at the end of November. Hence the President's announcement did not come until December 12.

When the announcement was made, Congressman Henry B. Gonzalez, in whose district the site was located, applauded the project and the President on the floor of the House. San Antonio was proud, he said, to have been chosen for this "imaginative" program. "Every day we can see why Lyndon Johnson of the Southwest is being described rightfully as the urban President of the 20th century." Within a month, Gonzalez had decided that he didn't like the project after all.

His change of mind began with a visit early in January to the commanding general of Fort Sam Houston, who told him that the decision to declare the land surplus had been handed down from Washington. The commander said that actually the Army needed the land. Gonzalez was quick to come to the defense of the fort, which, as headquarters of the Fourth Army and home of Brooke Medical Center, provided a large and growing number of jobs for his constituents. Gonzalez was also concerned about the suitability of the site for housing the poor. It was bounded on the northwest by the Missouri, Kansas and Texas Railroad and on the east by Interstate Highway 95. Army helicopters constantly flew over it. Gonzalez complained that the site would be dangerous, noisy, and dirty, and that it would be isolated from bus service and stores. Housing for the poor should be built nearer the center of the city, he argued, in the model cities area. A new town at Fort Sam Houston would "simply be an island of unhappy people, at sea in the very midst of San Antonio."

Gonzalez took various steps to thwart the project. He wrote to Quincy Lee, a San Antonio developer who was interested in it, to discourage him from participating. He visited Secretary of the Army Stanley Resor. Flying back to Washington from Texas on Air Force One, he appealed personally to the President. He wrote two letters to a member of the President's staff. And he issued press releases to the San Antonio papers.

Neither the White House nor HUD wanted to back down once the project had been announced, but they did not want to defy Gonzalez either. HUD had special grounds for concern inasmuch as he was a member of the Banking and Currency Committee, which handles housing and urban development legislation. At the President's instruction, Califano's office sought to arrange a meeting at which White House and HUD officials would try to persuade him of the project's merits. They were also prepared to let the Army retain thirty-two acres of the site for which the fort's commanding officer had proposed a specific, immediate use.

Perhaps on the theory that Gonzalez had been annoyed at not being included in the original announcement, White House staff members prepared to give him public credit when HUD announced award of survey and planning funds for the San Antonio project. Gonzalez, however—to the outrage of the White House staff member who was arranging all this—declined to come to the meeting. "Perhaps we should cancel the whole thing with an appropriate blast," the staff member suggested to Secretary Weaver. Instead Weaver had his special assistant for congressional relations call on the congressman, apparently with some success. By the end of March, Gonzalez had ceased active opposition.

One reason he relaxed may have been that the project wasn't making progress anyway. HUD's reply to Gonzalez had been that local officials and developers—presumably good judges of the prospects for success—were for the project, but it was becoming clear that official support was very weak. The mayor was not active on behalf of the project. At the time the urban renewal commission acted on the city's application for planning funds, some members were explicitly opposed. "Complainants literally were saying," the San Antonio *Light* reported, "that Fort Sam Houston was much more important to the city than any New Town In-Town project."

Although the urban renewal commission and the city council formally applied for survey and planning funds and HUD in April approved the application—a loan of $153,000—the city declined to spend the money. Deciding to leave planning to a developer, the urban renewal commission invited development proposals with advertisements in local papers and the *Wall Street Journal*, but it set no deadline for submission of proposals and none for choosing a developer. Months passed without progress.

Officials in HUD's central office grew impatient, but, lacking knowledge of the causes of delay, they were not sure what to do about it. Finally, as the anniversary of the President's announcement approached, McCabe called Jack D. Herrington, assistant regional administrator for renewal assistance, to ask him to meet with local officials and get an explanation. Herrington's reply confirmed that there was no local support for the project. Councilmen believed that the land should not be "pirated" from the Army and foresaw serious problems, such as lack of public transportation, in developing it for low-income residential use.

The urban renewal commission was unwilling to recommend the project to the council, and Herrington himself was unwilling to support it. He argued that HUD had forced the city into something it did not want to do (HUD of course had been compelled to act by the President), and was partly to blame if the city backed down. Reflecting on Herrington's behavior, Clinton thought that it was but one example of a general weakness of the program. He wrote to McCabe:

The lack of substantial progress in San Antonio, and some other cities, I believe, can be explained partially by the attitude evidenced by the Regional Office. The SLCD program is simply not getting the support it needs on the regional level. Projects of this nature need careful promotion and an extensive educational campaign to have a fighting chance of succeeding. Lacking these, a city's attitude could hardly be different from that evidenced thus far by San Antonio.

We have used our resources in this case to little or no avail. The Region's attitude seems to be that this is a "fad" program which will go away if ignored and this lack of response is not unique to this regional office. I think we must face up to the need for substantial central office involvement and guidance if this project is to be saved and if we are to move decisively on other projects elsewhere.

In December the city council voted not to proceed with the project, but rather than accept defeat HUD's central office began to explore the possibility of disposing of the land directly to a developer. Clinton proposed this course to Wood early in January as the Johnson Administration was drawing to a close, and appealed to HUD's budget office for an allocation of funds so that the surplus lands' office in Washington could administer a competition for developers.[1] Clinton pointed out to Wood, though not to the budget office, that this method of administering development would itself be innovative, and *ipso facto* would serve the goals of the program. Wood took no action on the suggestion; the budget office, after delay, referred the request for funds to the office of the undersecretary on the ground that it raised a major policy issue: when the local community did not wish to exercise initiative in the surplus lands program, should the federal government do so? Before the undersecretary could reply, the question was rendered moot by the failure of the project.

Local interest in developing the site had not expired completely. Although the city council was opposed to residential development, it resolved to designate the site for industrial use. In the spring of 1969 several members of the Chamber of Commerce went to Washington to propose this to Clinton. Still hoping to salvage something for his program, Clinton in turn made a trip to San Antonio in the summer to urge the urban renewal commission and the city council to consider using the site to experiment with new housing technology under the Nixon Administration's Project Breakthrough.

The revival of prospects for development revived the opposition of Gonzalez, who wrote HUD Secretary George Romney and Army

1. As the Johnson Administration ended, Steiner withdrew as director of the program and Clinton took charge.

Secretary Resor urging that the site be returned to Army control. When Clinton visited San Antonio, Gonzalez sent a telegram to Winston Martin, the urban renewal director, urging him to stand firm against HUD's pressure for housing development, and to save the land for the "long-range mission" of Fort Sam Houston. As Clinton requested, the city council did reconsider its position on development of the site; but the result was that it rejected again—for the last time—HUD's request to build housing. On August 21, the council formally resolved to ask the federal government to remove the land from the surplus list and restore it to the fort.

HUD's central office exchanged letters of appreciation and regret with two San Antonio developers, Quincy Lee and H. B. Zachry, who had maintained an interest in the project to the end. "In my opinion," Lee concluded, "this decision [to cancel the project] was made . . . at the request of Congressman Gonzalez. . . ."

4 ATLANTA:

Progress Through Pragmatism

The White House today announced plans to transform surplus Federal land into [a model community] in . . . Atlanta.

The new community in Atlanta will be located on a 95-acre surplus Department of Justice tract. The property is adjacent to the Thomasville Urban Renewal Project and near the Atlanta business district. When completed the community will include 400 housing units for poor and middle income families, parklands, schools and light industrial area.

White House News Release, December 12, 1967

ATLANTA WAS the only city in which the program did not meet frustration promptly. It was also the only one in which the city government was already committed to a program of housing construction for the poor. And even there, despite the promise of the planning stage, development was repeatedly delayed.

A survey team recommended three sites in the Atlanta area for consideration by the task force. Two of these were outside the city, and HUD rejected them because DeKalb County, whose government would have jurisdiction, did not have an approved workable program for community development and therefore could not qualify for federal development assistance. Also, federal officials doubted that the county government would agree to racial integration. The third site, known as "Honor Farm I," was vacant land within Atlanta, four miles southeast of the city center, adjacent to the Atlanta Federal Peni-

47

tentiary. It had been declared surplus by the Department of Justice.

A federal planning team met on October 24 with Mayor Ivan Allen and other Atlanta officials to explain the background of the program and the survey team's choice of sites. Allen was enthusiastic and said that the city would like to acquire Honor Farm I as soon as possible. The city planning department would begin at once to prepare an action program.

Although the city did not actually submit its program until December 22, the task force recommended early that month that the President announce the Atlanta project. Three months had passed since the announcement of Fort Lincoln, and Task Force Chairman Knott feared that the Defense Department would cease to cooperate in making land available unless the program seemed to be getting somewhere. In order to assure actual progress, it was essential to create the appearance of progress. The San Antonio and Atlanta projects were announced simultaneously.

At this stage the Atlanta project met no local opposition. The mayor was committed to a five-year program to build 16,800 houses for low- and moderate-income use, and the Honor Farm project promised to help meet this goal. Because the local program had been slowed by neighborhood opposition, zoning problems, and high land costs, the surplus lands project was especially welcomed as one that might avoid such obstacles. The Atlanta *Constitution*, which had applauded the program at the time of the President's announcement, did so again when Atlanta became involved, calling it "a fine opportunity" for the city. Rodney Cook, chairman of the urban renewal policy committee of the board of aldermen, participated in the Atlanta Housing Authority's planning sessions for the project and predicted a prompt start of construction. The board of aldermen stipulated that a substantial part of the housing at Honor Farm should be for the lowest income group. In short, there was strong support in Atlanta for low-income housing in general and at Honor Farm specifically.

Nor was there opposition at this point from neighbors. There could be no protest from the northwest, where the federal penitentiary sat. To the southeast lay the 267-acre Thomasville urban renewal project, just approaching completion, that had been developed with single-family, one-story houses selling for $12,000–$15,000. The buyers were blacks. Across McDonough Boulevard to the northeast, the regional office reported, were "minimum-standard houses occupied by prison guards and Chevrolet assembly plant workers, and by a site for low-rent public housing." This area too was black. To the southwest lay the Lakewood residential section, a "homogeneous neighborhood of older frame houses, occupied by community-centered, church-oriented, politically conservative, blue-collar workers." But this white neighborhood, which might otherwise have been aroused by the project, was separated from it by the Southern Railway and the Southview Cemetery.

The problems at Honor Farm were problems of planning more than of politics. In several respects the site fell short of the standards of community development to which HUD was committed.

For one, it was too small for creation of a new town, and too small even for the more modest development that the Atlanta Housing Authority envisioned. The authority's plan necessitated acquisition of an additional twenty-three acres from the Department of Justice. After some hard bargaining with the warden of the prison via Justice Department headquarters in Washington, HUD's central office managed to get the extra acreage.

A second problem was that the Georgia highway department was planning to run a superhighway, a connector between Interstate 485 and the Lakewood Expressway, through the middle of the site. Planning would be delayed until the department determined an exact location. Worse, no matter what the precise location, the 300-foot-wide swath of concrete through the site would be a travesty of the planning conception HUD was trying to promote. After reviewing the Atlanta action program, Dorn C. McGrath, director of HUD's Division of Metropolitan Area Analysis, sent Steiner anguished comments about this "brutal division of an integral site." He had thought that "land for housing rather than land for highways was Atlanta's critical need." The Atlanta plan was "unseemly" at a time when highway planning was being criticized country-wide "for its emphasis on cheap right-of-way rather than on community social and aesthetic values." He urged that other locations for the connector be considered. The reply from HUD's regional office in Atlanta, to which Steiner forwarded McGrath's memo, said that not building any connector was "out of the question politically" and defended the highway department's choice of a route as reasonable.

Finally, there was the question of the project's environment. The HUD planners' emphasis on "community" could lead, in the case of large sites (as at Fort Lincoln) to measures to differentiate development from surrounding areas, but in the case of smaller ones (as at Honor Farm) it implied measures of integration with the surroundings. McGrath's memo criticized the Atlanta action program for failing to show how this would be done. The regional office, in a slightly caustic reply, pointed out that the Honor Farm site was bordered on one side "by the high gray walls" of the penitentiary and on another by "the double-track main line" of the Southern Railway, environmental features that obviously defied integration. The regional office predicted that the new development and the Thomasville urban renewal project would benefit each other. "The Thomasville residents will feel themselves a part of the NTIT community, even though the Honor Farm site will have higher architectural and land-use standards. The pride of home ownership felt by Thomasville residents will motivate tenants in the Honor Farm site. Inversely, the middle-income families who will live in the Honor Farm site will make an impact on the aspirations of the Thomasville residents." Having made these reassuring statements for the benefit of the central office, the regional office went back to its business, which it conceived to be the promotion of development.

More than HUD's other regional offices, that in Atlanta took an interest in the program. The regional administrator assigned a staff member to it nearly full time, and the assistant administrator for renewal assistance, John T. Edmunds, became deeply involved in the project in Atlanta. "You get fast handling if the [assistant regional administrator] so desires," one central official noted, citing Edmunds as an example. The regional office's commitment was in part a reflection of the commitment of local officials. If Atlanta wanted to build something, the regional office would help it find a way.

The main problem for local and regional officials was the organization and financing of development. They wished to use the urban renewal program, but this course presented difficulties. They could not undertake an open land project because Georgia law prohibited it. As an alternative—more appealing anyway, because it would yield federal grants—they were tempted to add the Honor Farm site to the neighboring Thomasville renewal project, which was still active. The trouble with this was that McCabe, as deputy assistant secretary for renewal assistance, objected.

The urban renewal program was under attack for failing to complete projects expeditiously, and McCabe did not want to prolong the Thomasville project if he could avoid it. He also did not want to spend urban renewal funds. He had consistently maintained that such funds should not be used to write down land acquisition costs in surplus lands projects, preferring instead that GSA reduce its asking price. In the Atlanta case he went farther, and stipulated that there should be no capital grant for any purpose, not even site improvements. He hoped to experiment with an untried method—sale of the land, with use controls attached, directly from GSA to a private developer, who might then qualify for federal aid under HUD's program of mortgage insurance for development of large tracts.

McCabe gave in when Steiner's office argued that an urban renewal grant, as a tried and familiar technique, was the only way to make rapid progress in Atlanta. Like surplus lands administrators, McCabe felt pressure from the White House to produce results somewhere, and Atlanta was the best prospect. Without having settled on a development method, federal and local officials had staged a groundbreaking in May on a three-acre parcel there. Two months later, McCabe approved a capital grant increase of $1,429,000 for Thomasville, all but $100,000 of which was attributable to the new community.

In getting funds from the Renewal Assistance Administration, regional officials had help from the surplus lands project office in Washington, but they were not in close touch with that office for other purposes. Central supervision remained ineffective, nearly nonexistent, as the project proceeded.

"We are just not on top of what is or is not going on in the localities," Clinton complained to a staff member in September, citing Atlanta as well as San Antonio. The Atlanta Housing Authority had invited development proposals during the summer and would soon open the bids, but HUD's central office had not even seen an invitation let alone reviewed the instructions to competitors. The Housing Authority had picked a five-man jury from outside the city to judge the submissions. Whatever their expertise, these men had no occasion to be familiar with HUD's standards for development of surplus lands projects. In judging the competition they applied criteria stated by the Housing Authority, which were very brief and general ("excellence of the site plan for the development of the land . . . , excellence of the architectural design and quality of the proposed construction," etc.). These criteria may have been slightly influenced by federal guidelines. For instance, they said that the objective was "to serve a cross section of social and economic groups," but they incorporated the stipulation of the board of aldermen that "a substantial portion of the housing (at least 300 units)" must be for families of the lowest income group.

After the city had made the award, Clinton asked the regional office for an analysis of how the winning proposal (submitted by the National Homes Corporation of Lafayette, Indiana) would serve the objectives listed in the city's action program. The program included, for example, the following goals which had been inspired by HUD's guidelines: achievement of racial balance, retention in the community of families "which have moved upward in income and education, to serve as examples of success for others to imitate"; provision of schools "which will be recognized city-wide as superior"; and provision of a small neighborhood shopping center "for convenience and for development of community spirit." The regional office replied with a memorandum by the chief of its project planning and engineering branch, Thomas A. Ficht, which evaluated the NHC proposal according to conventional engineering and architectural criteria such as density of development and adaptation to topography.

For the next four months, from early February to early June 1969, the central office asked the regional office for an evaluation that would address the goals stated in the action program. Ficht, it turned out, had never seen a copy of HUD's development standards and he could see no point in preparing more evaluation in February of a proposal that the city had approved in December and that he had already evaluated according to the only criteria he felt competent to apply.

He did not pay much attention to what the action program said about racial balance, upward mobility, community spirit, and similar concerns originating from HUD's central office. Not until the central office sent a staff member to Atlanta to appeal to regional officials in person did Ficht supply a second memorandum, and it was scarcely more satisfactory than the first. Although it set forth the social objectives in the action program, it said very little about how they were to be achieved and nothing at all about racial balance in particular.

The regional office's attitude toward racial balance was one more example of its readiness to adapt to local realities, as with its acceptance of the highway route. Edmunds later explained, "We wanted to have the site developed in the most advanced way that could be sold to people in Atlanta. You go for what's possible, plus ten percent." He added that the regional office was more optimistic about achieving racial integration than class integration.

As of the fall of 1971, site improvements had been made but construction had not been started.

Delay occurred first because the National Homes Corporation, having underestimated the cost of housing construction by about $2 million, was unable to get a commitment of mortgage insurance from the Federal Housing Administration. It took a year of negotiation, along with an appeal by the Atlanta Housing Authority to HUD Secretary George Romney, before financing could be arranged. In the summer of 1971, after that problem was resolved, the AHA staged a groundbreaking—the project's second; the developer took title to the land; and construction crews prepared to start.

At the last minute, a lawsuit stopped them. Neighborhood opposition, which had not troubled the Atlanta project before, arose. A half dozen residents of the southeast section of the city filed suit in federal district court to enjoin the project, charging that it would result in excessive concentration of housing for the poor. A HUD directive in 1968 had ordered cities to disperse public housing, and a series of federal court decisions had confirmed and enlarged this rule, extending it in one case to other kinds of federally subsidized housing. Neighborhood residents now seized on this developing federal doctrine in an effort to protect themselves against a federally sponsored project. Fear of the surplus lands project had apparently increased as occupancy of the Thomasville project rose, and with it the population of the area's schools. The suit charged that the Honor Farm project did not provide for new schools.

In the fall of 1971, the AHA was preparing its defense and the developer was awaiting the court's decision.

5 LOUISVILLE:

Race and Other Obstacles

Secretary Robert C. Weaver of the U. S. Department of Housing and Urban Development today announced that a new community would be created on Federal surplus land in Louisville, Kentucky.

This is the fourth city in which unused military and other surplus Federal properties will be converted to new vital and useful community resources. . . .

The Secretary said the future Louisville new community will be known as Watterson Model Town. Located about four and a half miles south of the center of the city, the new community will occupy most of the 96 acres of the former Nichols General Hospital.

HUD News Release, June 27, 1968

THE GOAL OF racial integration was sufficiently controversial that it alone might have thwarted new towns in-town. That it does not figure more importantly in the cases described here may be accounted for in several ways. One is that HUD, as the Atlanta case shows, was prepared to put action ahead of integration on its list of priorities. Another is that some local officials, upon being informed of the importance of this goal, declined to participate in the program, although of course they did not give that as the reason for their lack of interest, and probably in no case was it the sole reason. A third explanation is that the task force deliberately avoided cities in which racial conflict was particularly active or intense. In December 1967, a prime site in Milwaukee was rejected for that reason. In Louisville racial conflict did not seem an obstacle until after the city had been picked by the task force.

Among five sites inspected by a survey team in Louisville, only one—what remained of the land for a Veterans Administration hospital—appeared to have potential for development. It consisted of fifty acres, the Nichols Army Support Facility, about a mile and a half from Churchill Downs Race Track in a white low- and lower-middle-income area of the city. It contained about forty war-time frame buildings in poor condition, the presence of which would easily qualify the site for urban renewal assistance. They were being used for reserve activities and armed forces entrance examinations.

On a visit to Louisville early in February 1968, a planning team found that Mayor Kenneth A. Schmied wanted to obtain the land for low- and moderate-income housing, and encouraged the mayor to have the city's urban renewal agency apply for survey and planning funds. It was the mayor's opinion, the planning team reported, "that this particular area would experience no racial problems and it was an appropriate area to build integrated housing." The city government was interested in putting up new housing to receive persons displaced by other public projects. After giving his assurances about the city's intent, the mayor in turn sought and received assurances that federal action would occur "in an expeditious manner."

One reason that federal offcials looked favorably on Louisville was that it had a large and active urban renewal program, with two projects completed and seven in execution. "Renewal has been the salvation for Louisville," a HUD position paper declared, "stimulating the first new construction in the downtown area since the 1920s." To be sure, this activity had not improved the housing situation of the poor. Much more housing had been destroyed than built, but the same could be said of urban renewal in other cities. There were also charges from within the city that renewal was increasing segregation. Just before leaving for Louisville as head of the planning team, a HUD renewal official learned that a complaint had been received from a local group, the West End Community Council, criticizing the mayor's appointments to the Louisville Human Relations Commission and charging that Alpha Gardens, a residential development in a renewal area, would be segregated. The complaint asked HUD to cut off assistance to the city. The planning team saw in this report a reason for pursuing a surplus lands project. A new town development, it reported—if "approached in good will by all parties concerned"—might "do away with existing racial tensions." In other words, an integrated project might be just what the city needed under the circumstances.

There were some obvious problems of site acquisition. The Defense Department was willing to part with only forty of the fifty acres. It planned to use the other ten for a new reserve center, but according to the Defense member of the planning team, it was willing to trade with the city for a comparable tract elsewhere. Even with fifty acres the site would be small for a new community. The survey team therefore recommended acquiring another thirty-five acres, part of the original hospital site, that the federal government had conveyed in 1961 to the Jefferson County Board of Education. Noting that the school board was using this property to store buses and supplies, the survey team concluded that it was "underutilized" and should be sought for housing, and the mayor agreed. In addition there was an adjacent tract of eleven acres, also part of the original site, that the Kentuckiana Children's Chiropractic Center was using for treatment of patients. Federal and local officials, concluding that the old wooden buildings were "barely satisfactory" for that purpose, hoped to recapture that tract too.

There would also be some problems in development. On a trip to Louisville in April, Clinton found that the urban renewal director, Jack D. Leeth, was concerned about providing the new community with shopping facilities and transportation. Leeth also thought that neighborhood opposition might be a problem. News accounts of the project in Louisville had provoked several protests to the mayor from citizens who objected to low-income housing and to the increased burden on neighborhood facilities. None of these problems, however, seemed insurmountable to local officials, and during April and May they proceeded, with the help of a planning consultant from Memphis, to prepare an action program and an application for survey and planning funds.

The Louisville project, when announced by the Johnson Administration in late June, was in some respects farther along than earlier projects had been at the time of their announcement. HUD's Renewal Assistance Administration had already approved a survey and planning grant of $267,552 and made a capital grant reservation of $1,066,000. However, in one potentially critical respect—that of land assembly—it was less far along. The ninety-six-acre figure used in the press release had been arrived at by adding forty, ten, thirty-five, and eleven, but only the first forty were certain to be available.

Once again, officials in Washington were eager to make a fresh announcement in the hope of accelerating the rest of the program. Undersecretary Wood, forwarding the draft press release to Weaver, recommended approval "as a means of increasing D. C. disposition to action." That the program was slowing down was clear from the nature of the press release itself. It came from HUD because the White House had declined to issue it.

In Louisville, in contrast to Atlanta, the local reception was poor. Whereas the Atlanta *Constitution* had welcomed Honor Farm as "a fine opportunity," the Louisville *Courier-Jorunal* was skeptical and sarcastic about Watterson Model Town. Barely a week after HUD's announcement it reported that much of the land for the new town was not actually available, that the project had been launched at federal rather than local initiative, and that its prospects for success were far less than Secretary Weaver's announcement made them seem. In an editorial, the paper charged that the city was planning such a project only because it had risen to the bait of federal cash. Two weeks later, still more harshly, it attacked the project as "a grandiose scheme" and asked why local officials were willing to attempt it and why HUD was willing to finance it. "It is almost as if the people in Washington want to build some sort of showcase, any sort, that will look good in an annual report on HUD activities." Also in contrast to Atlanta, there was opposition within the board of aldermen. Two members, including the president, had voted against the survey and planning application.

The *Courier-Journal* was correct in questioning the availability of land. Neither the county board of education nor the chiropractic center was willing to give up what it had. School Superintendent Richard Van Hoose told a reporter that every building on the site, "the school system's central maintenance and supply center," was being used to capacity. Van Hoose conceded that the mayor had contacted him informally about a transfer two or three months before HUD's announcement, but none had been agreed to. In August, when Leeth sat down with the school board to make the request, the answer was a flat "no." Dr. Lorraine Golden, administrator of the chiropractic center, had learned from the newspapers that city and federal officials wanted its land for a model town. As a chiropractic organization, the center would have found it difficult to get federal financing for a new building. To give up its present quarters, HUD's regional office reported to Washington, might be tantamount to dissolution.

Only with the greatest difficulty, after repeated meetings and exchanges of correspondence and with help from HUD's central office, did the city succeed in getting even the ten acres that the Army was supposed to be willing to trade. The effort exasperated the mayor, who hoped on the basis of assurances from the planning team that he would not meet procedural obstacles at the federal level. He probably would not have met this one except that Defense Department headquarters, which had made the initial offer of a trade, had very little control over the district office of the Corps of Engineers, which was in charge of building a reserve center and with which the negotiations over a trade had to be conducted.

In the months following HUD's announcement, the project made no progress. HUD's central office, believing that acquisition of the additional land was the main problem, awaited the outcome of negotiations. As of mid-October city officials still had not acknowledged defeat even though the negotiations were not getting anywhere. Then, on a visit to Louisville, a regional official concluded that the underlying obstacle—one that would remain no matter what the size of the site—was the local officials' fear of racial conflict. Mayor Schmied, who in February had been willing to risk introduction of blacks into the model town area, was no longer willing to do so. In the meantime several black riots had occurred in the city, and the project now seemed "so racially sensitive," the regional official reported, that neither the mayor nor the aldermen nor the urban renewal commissioners had any enthusiasm for it.[1] He later wrote, "They all would be glad for the Federal Government, acting alone, to get the model new town in-town built and labelled a federal undertaking, but they don't want to be a party to the undertaking."

Not for the first time, the central office faced the question of what to do when local officials lost interest in a project. Louisville differed from San Antonio in that it did not formally withdraw. Privately Leeth broached to Clinton the possibility of putting up a large amount of 221(d)(3) housing, which would be "more prudent" than "an experimental new community." This apparently was a euphemistic way of saying that the city would go ahead if it did not have to promise integration, although technically, of course, open housing and other civil rights legislation would apply as much to an "ordinary" project as to an "experimental" one. Throughout 1969 there was still no progress and when HUD's central office tried in October to schedule a field visit, Leeth asked for a postponement until after the mayoralty election of November 4. Nothing could be decided until then anyway.

The newly elected mayor, Frank W. Burke, expressed interest in the project. In 1970 the urban renewal agency completed planning, with results "a little better than prosaic," according to a federal official. It also found a developer. However, as progress occurred, neighborhood opposition revived and slowed approval by the board of aldermen. Not until July 1971 did the aldermen authorize the project.

It appeared thereafter that development of some sort would occur in Louisville, but HUD had long since ceased to expect the model new community that at first it had sought.

1. On this point, the interpretation of federal and local sources differs. Urban Renewal Director Leeth, asked by The Urban Institute to comment on this chapter, could not recall that local officials had ever expressed fear of racial conflict. He also emphasized that the mayor had not tried to promote integrated housing in the first place. According to Mr. Leeth: "The term 'integrated housing' is incongruous because of the fact that the City of Louisville had adopted and was enforcing a 'fair housing ordinance' long before the new town program was conceived. Mayor Schmied's enthusiasm for the project was motivated by his strong desire to help meet the city's critical housing needs for low and moderate income families. 'Race relations' as such had little, if anything, to do with his determination for the city to pursue this program."

6 CLINTON TOWNSHIP:
A Try at Private Action

The U. S. Department of Housing and Urban Development today announced the fifth undertaking in a program launched by President Johnson last summer to transform surplus Federal land into vital new communities.

Secretary Robert C. Weaver said the new community will rise on unused Federal property in Clinton Township, Michigan, in the Detroit metropolitan area.

HUD News Release, July 11, 1968

THE CLINTON TOWNSHIP PROJECT promised to serve well the federal aim of doing things in new and different ways. A private, nonprofit corporation that independently shared many of HUD's goals took charge of development. If the project should succeed, it would be because of the resourcefulness of this organization. There proved to be no magic, however, in bypassing a public agency for a private one.

The Clinton Township site was slow to become active. Its small size, fifty acres, and the obscurity of its location, roughly twenty miles northeast of Detroit, discouraged Washington's interest. Not until late February did the central office ask the region to find out whether local officials were interested in development. The answer was "yes."

Clinton Township is a rapidly growing bedroom suburb many of whose residents work in automobile plants in Warren. In 1968, most of its population of 32,000 was concentrated in the southern half of the township, but a sewer and water extension program gave promise of facilitating development in the north where the surplus site lay. The site itself was an off-base installation of Selfridge Air Force Base, of which twenty-nine acres were already excess and twenty-one acres were not. The two parcels were divided by a highway. Once again, there was no possibility of creating a full-fledged model new town, but local officials were enthusiastic at the prospect of low-income housing, which they hoped would facilitate relocation from an urban renewal project they were planning. The site was bounded on the west by an area of single-family houses occupied by moderate-income whites; on the north by a railroad spur and trailer park; on the east by an industrial area in which the dominant use was a scrapyard; and on the south by a settlement of poor blacks. The township government hoped eventually to carry out an urban renewal project in the black area, and again thought of the surplus lands project as a way of facilitating relocation. The long-standing presence of blacks in Clinton Township (about 2,000 of the residents were nonwhite) encouraged HUD, for it seemed to increase the prospect of achieving racial integration.

That the township government had experience with federal aid programs—public housing, sewer, and water projects were active, and an urban renewal application was pending—also encouraged HUD. Nevertheless, the assistant regional administrator for renewal assistance was very concerned, a central official noted, "about this untutored little town getting screwed by some redeveloper who will do a mediocre, badly planned job." Local officials would "need the money, advice and brainpower to cope with big developers." Where, the regional office asked, would these come from? The central office proposed that they come from the Metropolitan Detroit Citizens Development Authority (MDCDA).

MDCDA had been founded by Walter Reuther, president of the United Auto Workers, as a nonprofit corporation to promote construction and eventually the mass production of low-cost housing. Incorporated in 1966, MDCDA did not become active until after the riot in Detroit in the summer of 1967. Then it got money from New

Detroit, the businessmen's coalition formed to help the central-city poor. Leaders of Detroit business, educational, religious, and civic organizations served as officers; Reuther, as chairman, remained dominant. The executive director was a former member of the Michigan senate, Edward J. Robinson. Hortense Gabel of New York, formerly a city housing official there; Jack Conway of Washington, D.C., former deputy administrator of the Housing and Home Finance Agency and deputy director of the Office of Economic Opportunity; and OSTI, the Organization for Social and Technical Innovation, of Cambridge, Massachusetts, served MDCDA as consultants.

In April 1968, Clinton suggested to the regional office and Clinton Township officials that MDCDA be engaged to develop the surplus lands site. He and David Epstein, who was handling the project for the regional office, met with Robinson early in May to see if MDCDA would be interested.

Epstein was concerned that MDCDA had no record of performance. "It has undertaken substantial commitments," he reported to a superior in the region, "but there are no completed projects to serve as a basis for evaluation." Nevertheless, after the meeting and a study of the organization's credentials, Epstein and Clinton were satisfied that it could do the job. Robinson had assured them that it wanted to.

They then met with township officials—the supervisor, treasurer, and director of the housing authority—to get agreement to the arrangement. These officials sought assurance that the local government would not lose control over the project; they feared that MDCDA might fill the housing with Detroit families displaced by the riots. They understood that racial integration was a federal goal and did not dissent, but they wanted to use Clinton Township's housing for Clinton Township's blacks and not for Detroit's. When Epstein assured them that housing priority for township residents would be written into the development agreement, they accepted the MDCDA. The township's action program, which it had prepared earlier with the help of a planning consultant, was amended to provide that the federal government would sell the land directly to a private developer (understood to be MDCDA), subject to the local government's approval of the developer's plan. HUD then announced the project.

From that point on, the initiative lay with MDCDA. With no prodding from Washington, it submitted a development proposal that was exceptionally faithful to HUD's goals. MDCDA's fidelity, moreover, was not the kind that comes from mere paraphrasing of guidelines, but seemed to convey independent commitment. Did HUD want new technology? Promotion of new technology was the authority's very reason for being. Racial balance? "Everything must be done . . . ," the proposal said, "to make the community attractive to white and black, and then it must be advertised and sold with a marketing strategy that will achieve a balanced community. To this end, MDCDA will create early in the planning stage a marketing advisory committee composed of top flight, sensitive and visionary marketeers." In its other projects, MDCDA had already demonstrated a commitment to citizen participation. It promptly sent a staff member to Clinton Township to organize community meetings and appeal to the residents to participate in planning for the surplus lands site. In MDCDA, HUD's central office had found a local partner thoroughly committed to its objectives—but could this partner produce housing?

At the local level, the only important development problem seemed to be school construction. This required the cooperation of a neighboring school board, for most of the development would fall in the school district serving Mount Clemens, a city of 18,000 that lies within Clinton Township and serves as its business center. Actually, this situation may have been an advantage for the project in one respect. Clinton Township officials might have been less eager to proceed if responsibility for the school population had been theirs. Mount Clemens officials, though unhappy about the project, could do little to stop it. "Well, boys, it looks as though we have a housing development on our hands," the board president observed, at a meeting that Epstein attended. The Mount Clemens superintendent wrote a letter of complaint to President Nixon, and HUD officials briefly feared that they might get complaints from a congressman (they did not). In fact the school problem was resolved with relative ease.

MDCDA agreed to reduce the population density slightly and Mount Clemens agreed to add eight rooms to an existing elementary school.

MDCDA couldn't develop the site unless it could acquire the land, and HUD's first attempt at effecting a transfer—in the fall of 1969—failed in Congress. Under the Federal Property and Administrative Services Act of 1949, noncompetitive sales of federal land must be cleared with the Government Operations Committees. Other surplus lands projects either had not reached the point of land transfer or had relied on another law, Section 108 of the National Housing Act, which authorizes the secretary of Housing and Urban Development to dispose of federal land in urban renewal areas. This was the first time that clearance had been sought from the Government Operations Committees, and the Senate committee would not accept HUD's justification.

The committee plainly did not trust HUD to get the highest possible price for the land; MDCDA's offer of $114,200 was based on an appraisal by the Detroit office of the Federal Housing Administration, a component of HUD, and represented "the fair market value based on the highest and best use for which the site can be utilized," HUD explained. Had the submission and the appraisal come from GSA, as was customary, the committee might have accepted them; they did not come from GSA because it refused to accept the FHA appraisal. More fundamentally, GSA was reluctant to take responsibility for the submission because it did not want to jeopardize relations with the committee. Congress presumably trusted GSA, on the basis of past performance, to get top-dollar for federal property, and GSA did not want to undermine that trust.

If less than the highest possible price were to be obtained, the committee wanted legal justification for the government's sacrifice, but because the surplus lands program had no foundation in law, HUD could cite none. Confronted with a series of hard questions from Committee Chairman John McClellan, HUD gave up on this method of transfer and chose instead to adapt the Clinton Township Project to Section 108 of the National Housing Act.

Even with the land, MDCDA could not build housing without

federal financing, and here again it was having trouble. In February 1969, Robinson had informed HUD's central office that it was time to arrange mortgage interest payments for the first housing units (to be built under Sections 235 and 236 of the Housing Act of 1968, which authorize cheap mortgage financing for low-income persons). "May we assume," he asked Clinton, "[that] your office will insure the availability of these reservations as needed?" The answer was that he could assume no such thing. Clinton told him to apply at his local FHA insuring office and to hurry up about it—funds for Section 235 and 236 programs were very low and claims were already being made on the next year's appropriations. Clinton had told the FHA's central office of MDCDA's request and had tried to invoke the priority claim of the surplus lands program, such as it might be, but the clear implication of his reply was that Robinson could not count on Washington for help.

A year later Robinson appealed again to the central office for the same purpose, and with even more discouraging results. Unable to get Section 236 funds from the district office, he made a trip to Washington. An FHA official there told him, in the presence of a member of Clinton's staff, that surplus lands projects had no priority within FHA and that authority to fund FHA projects belonged entirely to the regional offices. Again—this time more firmly and to his face—Robinson was told to go back to the region and get in line.

Both of these cases illustrate Robinson's, as well as HUD's, method of working. As a former legislator, he felt at home in the world of politics and government, and his impulse when MDCDA needed action from the federal government was to rely on contacts in Washington. He had urged HUD to make the submission to the Government Operations Committees, and three weeks before this was to be done he assured members of Clinton's staff that "he had the wheels greased and ready in both houses. . . ." When the Senate committee balked, Robinson sought help from Reuther when Reuther was next to be in Washington, from the UAW's Washington lobbyist, and from both of Michigan's senators, but the committee remained firm. Similarly, when dealing with the administration, Robinson liked to work as near the top as possible. But "the top" in this case—Clinton's office, or even FHA in Washington—did not control the funds that MDCDA was seeking, and to bypass the regional office, which *did* control them, risked alienating regional officials.

Neither Clinton's office nor MDCDA gave up on the project. Both continued to press FHA for a commitment of mortgage insurance. Finally, in the fall of 1970, FHA approved 160 units, fewer than the 300 MDCDA had applied for, but enough to warrant a start on construction. Ground was broken in December for a complex of town houses. As of September 1971, occupancy of the first units was scheduled for November, and all 160 were expected to be ready by January 1. MDCDA had also applied to FHA for another 134 units.

Whether the new community would be completed continued to depend heavily on MDCDA's persistence and resourcefulness in dealing with the federal government and on its general competence as a developer, which had yet to be established. As of the fall of 1971, it had built only 600 housing units after four years of effort and expenditure of several million dollars. If the surplus lands project were completed, it would be one of MDCDA's first successes. And it would probably be the first success for the surplus lands program, for Clinton Township was the only place, four years after the program's founding, where construction was actually underway.

7 NEW BEDFORD:

A Mayor Retreats

Plans to create a new community in New Bedford, Massachusetts, using Federal and city-owned surplus land, were announced today by the U. S. Department of Housing and Urban Development.

New Bedford is the sixth city to take part in converting military and other surplus Federal properties into vital and useful community resources.

. . . Twelve hundred units of various types of housing are planned.

HUD News Release, July 25, 1968

UNLIKE OTHER new-town projects, that in New Bedford originated with the mayor, not federal officials. In a program that suffered from lack of local support, this might seem an advantage of critical importance, yet no project died faster than New Bedford's. Announced in July, it ended in October.

Late in February 1968, Mayor Edward F. Harrington wrote to HUD's surplus lands office to ask whether his city could participate in the program. The Office of Economic Opportunity was closing a Job Corps training center at Fort Rodman, an old army base in the southern part of the city, and the mayor had set up a committee of civic leaders to suggest a use for the site. The mayor pointed out that the area was already zoned for residential use and that the city was "a depressed area" with an unemployment rate over six percent and "a substantial lack of middle- and low-income housing."

This was typical of Harrington's enterprise as mayor. Since taking

office in 1962, he had shown a sharp awareness of federal aid programs. Like many manufacturing cities in New England, New Bedford had been declining economically since the 1920s. Harrington
sought to revive it with federal help.

Steiner sent Harrington's letter to the HUD regional office in New
York with a request that officials there explain the surplus lands program to the mayor and let headquarters know the result. The initial
contacts were encouraging, and late in April the city submitted an
action program. It had decided to combine city-owned land, what
remained of "the poor farm," with the Fort Rodman tract. Together
the two would amount to about 100 acres. Overlooking Buzzards
Bay, this was an excellent site.

The regional office submitted a favorable report on the action program, along with a glowing appraisal of the "municipal capability"
of New Bedford. It described the mayor as "strong," "resourceful,"
and "generally well-liked." His margin of victory in the past three
elections had averaged eight to one, and he had "a fine rapport with
the citizenry." The redevelopment director, city planner, and community action program director—"able, hard-working, and talented
public servants"—were "primarily responsible for the success of
New Bedford's sixty-odd federal and state programs during the past
seven years." The report also praised the city's record on civil rights:
"New Bedford has always had a reputation as an open city with em-
ployment and cultural activities for all. One of the first cities in New
England to employ black policemen and school teachers, New Bedford's municipal activities today are liberally sprinkled with nonwhite personnel. The Executive Secretary to the Mayor is nonwhite,
as is the Chairman of the Steering Committee of the Local CAP
Agency. . . ."

HUD headquarters approved the action program and announced
the project. Up to this point, it had received no more than one or
two casual indications that the project might run into trouble, and
these were counterbalanced with reassurance. Late in April Mayor
Harrington had called Clinton to clear with him the creation of a blue-
ribbon citizens committee to support the project, explaining that he
wanted to counteract opposition from citizens who lived near Fort

Rodman and "a certain element in the city council that represented them."

By late June, when HUD headquarters was reviewing New Bedford's action program, this problem had apparently passed. The regional office reported that the mayor "does not foresee any significant objection to the program on the part of the community. He relates that he has received phone calls from some persons in the immediate area, but these appeared to be calls of inquiry rather than protestation." Nor did he expect difficulty in securing approval from the city council. Neither the city nor HUD had been able to persuade the Army to give up part of the Fort Rodman site on which it planned to build a reserve training facility, but this problem was not serious enough to jeopardize the project.

After the project was announced the regional office forwarded another reassuring report, though it did not omit signs of trouble. "The announcement was greeted with much fervor and enthusiasm locally," it said. Mayor Harrington had seized the occasion to say he was totally opposed to a proposal of the city council president that the site be zoned for single-family dwellings only, an action that would kill the new-community project. "Mayor Harrington indicates," the report concluded, "that neither the City Council nor the Planning Board will be receptive to this bland attempt [sic] to undermine the 'FELCUN' program in New Bedford."

Meanwhile, HUD headquarters was hearing citizen protest directly. In July and August it received letters from twenty residents of the city's South End who objected to the project. A representative one, from Felix Hodziewich, said:

We live across from the "poor-farm" area, a nice grassy, quiet slope down to the water. This is the last property near the water in New Bedford and it would be a crime to construct garden apartments and a commercial component on it. When we bought our land, the deed stipulated residential [single-family] only, and it should either be made into a park, embraced by sea breezes for all residents of New Bedford to enjoy, or it should be sold into single family house lots—not become a "business district."

Within a three-block area containing 13 homes, there are three colored families living here and we hope they never move away. So this is a racially integrated area. But we all keep our homes clean and peaceful and wish it to stay that way. Our taxes are from $500–$800 a year and we are raising youngsters, and find it not too easy to accept this "poor-farm area" project that will involve an influx of crowds of people, traffic, noise, dirt, trucks, businesses, and so on into this area.

The mayor and 1,000 residents of the South End confronted each other at a meeting on September 10. The mayor tried to explain the project; the crowd demanded single-family houses. When Harrington asked for a show of support for multi-family dwellings, fewer than ten persons raised their hands. It was an emotional meeting, made more so by charges of racism. The United Front, the city's black militant organization, was supporting the project, and it claimed that the opponents in the South End were trying to keep blacks out of their area. When a United Front member at the meeting charged "bigotry and bias," about 100 persons walked out. "The issue of bias does not exist," one South End resident declared, drawing loud applause. "The people of the South End have been labelled by your office, Mr. Mayor, by the newspaper and radio stations. This is just not so." Most of the city councillors attended the meeting, but none spoke.

Two nights later, the city council voted to restrict the project site to single-family use. Only two councillors, of whom one was the mayor's brother, were opposed. About 300 South End residents jammed the chamber to watch the vote. The United Front was not there, but afterward its president said, "I don't think the black people of New Bedford will stand by and see this happen without raising hell." (Three percent of New Bedford's population is black.) Defending the council against the charge of racism, Councillor Daniel F. Hayes pointed out that it had long supported single-family zoning in the city. It had repeatedly rejected requests to rezone for apartments.

Mayor Harrington sought federal help in saving the project. Despite the council's action on zoning, he still intended to ask it to approve a planning grant application. Two days before the council meeting, Clinton, a member of HUD's regional office, and local planning and redevelopment officials met privately with council members to try to win their support. Clinton agreed to accept the mayor's invitation despite concern that HUD might be criticized for "undue interference with local government" (he solicited Under-secretary Wood's approval before accepting).

Before meeting with the council, the group had lunch with civic and business leaders. They seemed enthusiastic about the project and willing to put pressure on the council. The council, however, was cool, and on September 26 it defeated the mayor twice more. At a second hearing on the zoning action, it voted again—nine to one, this time—for the restriction to single-family use. And it defeated the planning grant application, eight to two.

The mayor was reluctant to give up. He told HUD that he would veto the zoning action and that with help from the newspaper and businessmen, he hoped to get the council to reverse its vote on planning funds. By the end of October, however, he had to admit defeat. He wrote to Clinton:

Apparently, all of our efforts have come to naught, and we have received a continuing ten to one negative vote against even a serious consideration of our town in-town project. At this time it seems that any consideration of the use of the Poor Farm and Fort Rodman property for this purpose is useless. I certainly regret the fact that minds in New Bedford were so narrow that we couldn't accomplish our goal to provide good housing and a major tax advantage for the City of New Bedford.

I herewith request that you bring to a conclusion all matters arising out of our inquiry for a New Town Project on this particular site.

8 SAN FRANCISCO:

A Victory for the Conservationists

The U. S. Department of Housing and Urban Development today announced plans to transform surplus Federal land in San Francisco, California, into two new community developments. . . .

The larger of the two San Francisco projects consists of 71 acres overlooking the Pacific Ocean and is located in the southwest corner of the city. . . .

The second site, totaling 12 acres, is in the northwest part of San Francisco, overlooking the Golden Gate Bridge. . . .

Preliminary plans call for both sites to be developed with housing and related facilities to serve families of various income levels. Full advantage will be taken of the extraordinary natural beauty of the sites. . . .

Secretary Weaver commended the personal leadership and enthusiasm of Mayor Joseph L. Alioto in advancing this development.

HUD News Release, September 13, 1968

THE NATURAL BEAUTY of San Francisco made it a prime location for a model new town. A survey team covered the Bay Area thoroughly and came up with two small yet superbly located sites. But if natural beauty was a planning asset, it was a political liability. What federal planners wished to exploit, local conservationists wished to preserve—and the local interests won.

The best site in San Francisco was at Fort Funston, seventy acres of an abandoned Nike battery in the southwest corner of the city, overlooking the ocean. The regional office described it as "generally a very buildable site, in an area relatively uncongested [and unmarked] with any particular racial or economic characteristics." The survey

75

team's other choice was a twelve-acre rectangular parcel at old Fort Miley, about six miles west of the central business district, close to the entrance to the Golden Gate bridge. Both the survey team and the regional office thought it would be an excellent place for housing unskilled employees and other low-income persons dependent upon the Fort Miley Veterans Administration Hospital. Both sites, because they contained concrete bunkers and other "improvements," would probably qualify for federal urban renewal assistance as predominantly open land.

Because San Francisco was having a mayoralty election in the fall, a federal planning team did not visit the city until January 1968. Then it found that the new mayor, Joseph L. Alioto, was interested in developing both sites. Alioto thought that the Fort Funston development in particular would help meet the city's need for relocation housing. He asked the planning and renewal agencies to work with HUD's regional staff in preparing an action program.

Thereafter things moved slowly in San Francisco. After two months had passed without the submission of an action program, HUD's central office asked the regional office to prod the city. The regional administrator wrote Alioto: "You are familiar I am sure with the President's interest in this program as a direct contribution to the solution of urban problems, and we are now in the position of needing to demonstrate that the potentials identified for utilizing this approval will produce real results. . . . May we hear from you soon? . . ." Still no action plan arrived.

Late in March the mayor's deputy for development, John Tolan, explained to the regional office that the autonomy of the city planning commission made it difficult for the mayor to act swiftly. Much of the planning was being done not by the city at all but by a prospective developer, Boise Cascade Company, drawn in by the mayor because he was at odds with the planning commission. An official of Boise Cascade called Clinton in April to assure him that the company was working diligently.

Still no action program arrived, and lack of progress—not only in San Francisco but elsewhere—was making it difficult for HUD to maintain a claim to the sites. In this case GSA wanted to build a records center on the Fort Miley site, which had already been declared excess[1]—a specific proposal was awaiting approval by GSA Administrator Knott—and the Defense Department was showing reluctance to part with the Funston site, which had not been declared excess. Surplus lands officials appealed to Undersecretary Wood, who happened to be planning a trip to San Francisco, to needle the mayor. They also appealed to city officials to take the offensive against GSA, preferably by a direct appeal to the White House. If the Miley site were to be saved for housing, only a show of local interest could save it.

All of this prodding did produce some results. The city (really, Boise Cascade) submitted an action program at the end of May. Although HUD's central office found it "extremely thin," rather than reject it the office prepared a supplement that Alioto signed during a visit to Washington. And GSA, after initial resistance to the city's appeals, agreed to leave the Fort Miley site to the surplus lands program. The matter was settled in late July at a meeting between Mayor Alioto and Administrator Knott. HUD then sent a draft press release to the White House (the department had continued to clear such releases with the White House and to hope that it would choose to issue them). Eventually it came back with a note from a presidential assistant: "Although the President approved release of this San Francisco project here, it has just sat in the press office for the past week. We have retrieved it, and in the interest of moving it along we think it best if you release it at HUD as soon as possible." It was issued on Friday, September 13.

So far there had been no active opposition in San Francisco. But central officials in HUD had had a premonition of what was to come. In mid-June, Clinton wrote to a staff member: "I was somewhat alarmed by [a HUD official's] comments (perhaps offhand) that Funston's highest and best use would be as a park—if history is to be our judge. Ask [him] directly if there is any way we can measure anticipated negative reaction from conservationists, Audubon Society

---

1. Federal land is "excess" when the specific occupying agency decides that it no longer needs the tract; land is "surplus" when no agency of the federal government wants it.

types, bird watchers, Izaak Walton Leaguers and other anarchists. Can he give us a judgment as to likelihood of concerted, serious opposition?????" The reply was: "Feels there will be opposition of some magnitude; feels we can get away with our plans but we'd better be ready to explain and justify."

When the announcement was made it provoked instant opposition, and no one in San Francisco was prepared to explain and justify the projects, plans for which had not progressed much beyond what HUD had found thin. A Defend the Forts Committee sprang up within twenty-four hours and held a press conference at which one speaker after another denounced the mayor's proposal. Simultaneously with the two surplus lands projects, the mayor had announced plans for a third, a luxury apartment development at Fort Mason in downtown San Francisco, which aroused the strongest opposition of all. The Funston and Miley projects suffered from association with Mason, which had no connection with the surplus lands program. Mason had been included at the insistence of the planning commission.[2]

Clinton, reading the press clippings out of San Francisco, noted anxiously that "the Ft. Lincoln and Ft. Rodman patterns could be repeated in San Francisco if Alioto does not act swiftly to create a supportive community organization." Alioto, however, was out of the city much of the time campaigning for the Democrats. Clinton urged his staff to get Tolan to combat the opposition right away, again adding, "We don't want another New Bedford."

At least in Washington, it was still not clear what or whom the opposition consisted of. A phone call to the regional office in early October identified two groups—one that was opposed to building low-rent housing on high-value property, the other that was opposed to building high-income housing at the expense of losing the sites for the poor (a complaint that must have been inspired principally by the Fort Mason project). "There is an overriding lack of knowledge about the projects by both," the caller concluded. City officials had been concerned about the first point themselves. In

2. Interview, Walter Rybeck of The Urban Institute with John Tolan, Washington, D.C., August 4, 1971.

April, when Steiner's office had been casting about for an explanation of the city's failure to act, an official elsewhere in HUD reported "some real doubts on the city's part as to whether they can put low- and moderate-income housing on a site [Funston] worth perhaps $30 million."

In order for the projects to proceed, the mayor had to request the Board of Supervisors, the city's legislative body, to rezone the sites for residential use. Tolan anticipated defeat—at least two of the supervisors had warned him that they were opposed—and tried to get a postponement, arguing that the board should hear testimony from prospective developers. The board refused, however, and then in mid-January unanimously rejected housing construction at Forts Miley and Funston. Instead it declared a preference for open space, and appealed to the federal government to remove the fences around Fort Funston and to refrain from building a records center at Miley. The board's action, the San Francisco *Chronicle* reported, was a victory for conservation groups, some of whose members had sat through twelve hours of board business in order to be present for the vote. It came at 3:00 a.m.

Shortly after the supervisors' action, Mayor Alioto notified the regional office that San Francisco was withdrawing from the surplus lands program. Soon after that, GSA notified the mayor that it was going ahead with a records center at Fort Miley. The conservationists' victory had been short-lived.

III · POST MORTEM

9 THE LIMITS OF CENTRALIZATION

FOUR YEARS after the start of the surplus lands program, only 120 units of housing had been built. At Fort Lincoln, where this housing stood, no other construction was under way. In Clinton Township, 160 units were being built. In Atlanta, a developer was ready to start, but was being delayed by a citizens' suit. In Louisville, approval had only recently been received from the board of aldermen. In San Antonio, New Bedford, and San Francisco, the projects had been cancelled. This chapter analyzes why the program produced so little.

Failure resulted mainly from the limited ability of the federal government to influence the actions of local governments and from its tendency to conceive goals in ideal terms. Both of these disabilities are associated with its place as the central government in the American federal system.[1]

1. Because society and government are complicated, social and political events are susceptible to many different interpretations. Were it to be explained fully, the failure of the surplus lands program would be seen to have had many causes. One was the relative inability of the poor to organize and to assert their interests. Another was the ability of local opponents to act effectively, which in turn is to be explained by the widespread dispersion of power and authority in American government and by a governmental tradition of responding to citizen pressure. Another cause is to be found in the great difficulty of organizing cooperative activity on a large scale. Even when local politics posed no insuperable obstacles to development, it was very hard to get anything done. Developers miscalculated costs, had trouble getting financing, or ran into some kind of procedural delay. The explanation advanced here, which focuses on the properties of American federalism, has been chosen because the author believes it to be the single most inclusive and illuminating explanation of many that might be explored.

To achieve many of its domestic purposes, including community development, the federal government relies on local governments.[2] However, because of the division of authority among governments in the federal system, the federal government cannot order these governments to do anything. It gets them to carry out its purposes by offering incentives in the form of aid, which they may accept or not, and by attaching conditions to the aid. To achieve results, federal officials must have enough knowledge of local politics to perceive what incentives are necessary; they must supply the incentives in sufficient quantity; and they must direct the incentives to those holders of local power whose support is required to achieve the federal purpose. In short, they must intervene successfully in local politics. They were unable to do this in the surplus lands program.

Limited Knowledge

The President's distance from local politics made it difficult for him to analyze the housing problem from the perspective of local officials, and to calculate the advantages and disadvantages of housing development as they would. "He did not understand," one of his aides later said, "what a mixed blessing low-income housing was for the cities."

The President and his staff believed that housing construction for the poor had run into trouble locally because of objections from those who would be displaced by development or from those whose neighborhoods the displaced would invade. If local officials were supplied with vacant land, they could produce housing. This analysis overlooked the extent to which objections arose from persons whose neighborhoods would be invaded by development, and it overestimated the desire of local governments to house the poor. What defeated the surplus lands projects locally was not different from what has defeated other attempts to build low-income housing: the pref-

2. The term "local" here is broad and inclusive; it refers to all those governments, conventionally called state and local, which are *not central*. In the surplus lands program, the governments with which the federal government dealt were local also in the narrower, more specific sense, as that level of the federal system which is neither federal nor state.

erence of local officials for types of development that will yield more tax revenue; their reluctance to act in the face of specific, intense opposition; and the absence of organized support.[3]

This flaw in conception might have been corrected as the program passed from the White House into the hands of the executive departments. HUD, where experience with urban development programs was concentrated, might have been sensitive to the prospect of resistance or indifference at the local level. However, rather than assessing the effectiveness of the means the program would employ, HUD concentrated on objectives of development; its first act was to prepare development standards. It took the basic means of bringing development about—offers of surplus land at low prices—as given. Federal officials generally assumed that these offers would be very effective.

That HUD formulated the objectives to call for model communities did not significantly alter the local officials' estimate of the federal proposal. It still required a large amount of housing for the poor, and —on top of that—race and class integration, superior public services, and technological innovation. Because development in these cases was to occur on a large scale, often on vacant land in remote parts of the city, local officials were probably more concerned than usually about having to develop public services, especially transportation and education. Otherwise, there was probably nothing that distinguished local resistance to these projects from resistance to other proposals for housing the poor. For the purpose of this account, which is to analyze the failure of a *federal* program, the main point is that federal officials failed either to anticipate these forces or to counteract them.

Because conditions affecting development—for example, the availability of federal land, the content of state laws, local experience with development programs, the leadership ability of the mayor, the responsiveness of the city government to the interests of the poor—could vary greatly from place to place, it might be argued that HUD

3. On the politics of public housing, see Leonard Freedman, *Public Housing: The Politics of Poverty*, New York, 1969, and Martin Meyerson and Edward C. Banfield, *Politics, Planning, and the Public Interest*, Glencoe, 1955. Freedman's book contains a bibliography.

would have found it very difficult to make in advance a general estimate of the program's prospects. It would have to judge the conditions in each city. In fact, this is what the department did, but even case-by-case it was unable to calculate the prospects of success correctly. It was unable to evaluate accurately the local officials' expressions of interest, and it was unable to anticipate either the development of local opposition or the willingness and ability of local officials to deal with opposition.

Again, distance from the scene and detachment from the conduct of local affairs were handicaps. HUD's central office had to rely for information on what planning teams and regional officials reported. They in turn had to rely on local officials, whose statements were often misleading. If the mayor of New Bedford said that he had the votes he needed in the city council, how were federal officials—those in Washington especially—to know better? To judge the prospects for local success required a very sophisticated system for gathering political intelligence, which HUD lacked. Besides, not even the most sophisticated intelligence system could have forecast accurately the amount, source, and timing of opposition. How could anyone have known that the Atlanta project, which had met no neighborhood opposition in four years, would be stalled at the last minute by a citizens' suit?

The introduction of federal benefits into the local political system has a number of effects which are difficult for either federal or local officials to anticipate accurately and which may or may not contribute to the achievement of federal purposes. It raises issues over whether the federal program should be undertaken; over who will benefit from the aid; and over how decisions are to be made for the program or project that is being aided, a result that the federal government itself has encouraged with citizen-participation requirements. Federal intervention is likely to mobilize a variety of local interests; federal administrators can only hope that more supporters of the federal purpose than opponents will be mobilized. The offer of aid does of course give supporters an advantage in the local contest.

The Limited Stock of Aid

That the supply of federal incentives was limited was a second cause of failure. To induce local governments to accept the burden of developing new towns in-town, the federal government had to give them something of value. The President assumed that low-cost surplus land would be available for this purpose, but this assumption turned out to be wrong.

Under pressure from the White House to put a program together in a hurry, administrative officials had jumped to the conclusion that the federal government could sell surplus land at a low price. However, lawyers from the executive agencies revised this assumption when they studied the question more carefully. In fact, sale at less than fair market value would have required a change in federal law. Having launched the surplus lands program on the assumption that it needed no new legislation, the Administration thereafter would not ask for any. HUD officials had to content themselves in 1968 with submitting one minor amendment for clearance by the Bureau of the Budget, a bill that would have facilitated below-market-value sales in a limited number of cases. The bill was never sent to Congress.

The program still might have been saved if local officials had been much interested in saving it. Even without a reduction in land price, the program gave local governments help with land assembly and relocation. Also, federal ownership of the land would relieve a developer of the interest charges and taxes normally incurred between the time of site acquisition and construction. If they had wanted to use the federal sites for housing, local officials might have asked Congress to help by authorizing disposal at less than fair market value. As of 1969, they were showing much interest in getting federal land cheaply for industrial development, but not much in getting it for housing. The surplus lands projects had aroused so little interest locally that few ever reached the point of land transfer and thereby encountered the obstacle of land cost.[4]

4. In 1969, no longer constrained by the Johnson Administration's injunction of no-new-legislation, HUD's surplus lands project office sought an amendment that would authorize sale of land for low- and moderate-income housing at a price based on reuse value rather than fair market value. The Bureau of the Budget removed this

Even if the federal government had been able to offer the incentives the President thought it could, HUD might not have been able to make the program work. It is not clear that land at a reduced price would have elicited the amount of local support that was necessary to realize the President's or HUD's objectives. A still more powerful incentive would probably have been required—perhaps *free* land, combined with very large subsidies for housing construction and for public facilities and services.

The Limited Uses of Aid

A third cause of failure was the limited ability of the federal government to use effectively such incentives as it possessed. Because it depended on local officials to be the agents of its purpose, whatever flaws there were in the local officials' ability to act effectively—to gather public support, to overcome opposition, to assemble an administrative organization—were liabilities for the federal government as well.

HUD tried to direct local governments to create their own support. At Steiner's suggestion, planning teams were supposed to urge the mayor to set up an "advocate force" in the city. Political support, however, rarely is generated by pure artifice. Where little support existed, a directive from HUD to the mayor could not create it. Besides, the mayor would do what HUD asked only if he were eager to have its aid. In the surplus lands program, the offer of aid was itself problematic, and the terms—creation of a model new community, containing much housing for the poor—were not very appealing. Local officials therefore were not amenable to federal direction.

Nothing could illustrate better the limited ability of the federal government to direct local affairs than the Johnson Administration's failure to make fast progress with Project One at Fort Lincoln.

That the District of Columbia is a federal city, that the President

---

item from HUD's legislative program, objecting that this was "backdoor spending." The Bureau maintained that the proper way to accomplish the purpose was with a direct program of appropriations for land purchase. The Senate Banking and Currency Committee put HUD's request back into the housing bill of 1969, and a much-qualified version was enacted.

appoints the mayor, that federal administrative officials can observe local events closely and even participate in them directly (as through HUD's membership in the Fort Lincoln staff committee)—none of these special circumstances sufficed to enable federal administrators to get Project One under way promptly. Impatient for action, they had to wait while the mayor dealt with his citizen-participation problem.

To get their groundbreaking, White House and HUD officials relied at first on exhortation to the mayor, but their use of this technique was circumscribed by a reluctance to get too deeply involved in local affairs and by an awareness of their own lack of knowledge of local politics. "You can't tell a mayor exactly what to do," a presidential assistant later said—meaning, apparently, both that it is improper to try, because the local sphere is rightly the responsibility of local officials, and that federal officials do not have enough knowledge of the local situation to try even if they should think it proper to do so. In the view of federal officials, it was the mayor's business to know how to get things done in his city. They would simply urge him to do something.

As the Johnson Administration neared an end, HUD resorted to a threat to withhold funds. (More precisely, it threatened to give to other cities funds that had been earmarked for Washington.) Although surplus lands was not a traditional grant-in-aid program, that Fort Lincoln would be developed with urban renewal and housing subsidies made the local government susceptible to such a threat. That HUD felt it necessary to resort to this technique shows how poor the federal government's stock of influence is. In view of the federal origins of the project, the threat amounted to saying, "We are so anxious for you to hurry with what we want you to do that if you don't hurry, we will prevent you from doing it at all."

In the end, the Administration did not withhold funds; on the contrary, the mayor extracted additional funds from it as the price of producing a groundbreaking by the Administration's deadline. He bought off citizen opposition with federal money.

In summary, one explanation for the failure of the program is that it lacked local support, or, more precisely, enough support to outweigh opposition. The federal government was unable either to anticipate this problem or to overcome it once the program was under way. Federal administrators could not control what happened in local politics because they had too little knowledge of it, too little right to intervene, limited resources with which to intervene, and limited ability to manipulate the resources they had.

This explanation applies well to the cancellation of projects in San Antonio, New Bedford, and San Francisco, the delay in Louisville, and much of the delay in Project One in the District of Columbia. Conversely, the existence of local support explains the *relative* success of projects in Atlanta and Clinton Township, which progressed with reasonable dispatch to the point at which construction might be started. These cases taken together suggest the proposition: the greater the local support for a project, the greater the likelihood of success.

In both Atlanta and Clinton Township, organizations with the backing of the municipal government (the Atlanta Housing Authority and MDCDA respectively) were prepared to promote development. In both, especially in Atlanta, the local organizations got strong support from the federal regional office. Local initiative was necessary in both cases to bring about federal as well as local action.

The federal government depends on local initiative to overcome some of its own disabilities, especially lack of coordination. For a local development project to be carried out requires specific contributions of support from various components of the federal government—in an extreme case, from Congress, several executive departments, and several operating units within HUD. At least in the surplus lands program, the federal government was unable to achieve coordination from "the top down"; instead, coordination had to come from "the bottom up," through the appeals of local officials. The lobbying activities of the director of MDCDA illustrate this process, although because they were not very successful, they do not illustrate it very well.

The trouble with the proposition stated thus far—that the degree of success depended on the degree of local support—is that it does not very well fit the leading case, Fort Lincoln. Development in the District of Columbia, with the partial exception of Project One, did not founder on local politics. Local officials as of 1969 wanted to go ahead with the new community project, and, despite the distractions of the citizen participation issue, no local interests were objecting. Some other explanation is required for the failure of Fort Lincoln.

The Inflation of Objectives

A final cause of the program's failure, which had more effect at Fort Lincoln than elsewhere, was that federal officials had stated objectives so ambitious that some degree of failure was certain. Striving for the ideal, they were sure to fall short. Worse, striving for the ideal made it hard to do anything at all.

The Fort Lincoln project got stalled mainly because neither federal nor local officials believed that the development plan was feasible. This plan, however, was quite faithful to the development guidelines that HUD laid down. If the plan would be very hard to carry out, that was because the goals would be very hard to achieve.

The goals of the surplus lands program were defined by HUD officials and consultants to HUD who were chosen to represent professions involved in urban development. The only local public official among them was the city manager of Tacoma, Washington, who was named because he was president of the International City Management Association. Logue, as principal development consultant for the pilot project, confirmed and elaborated the goals. He was chosen (by Appleby, with HUD's concurrence) not for any experience with the District of Columbia, but for skills that presumably were applicable anywhere in the country and commensurate with the demands of the pilot project of a national program. Whereas execution of the projects depended on local politics and administration, conception of the program and the definition of goals were independent of local activity; they occurred at the federal level.

The planners[5] of the surplus lands program and particularly of the

5. "Planners" indicates those who participated in HUD's definition of goals, either through the activities of the development standards team or through the planning of Fort Lincoln. Not all the "planners" were members of the city planning profession, though many were. The term here excludes the President and members of the White House staff, whose conception of the program was independent of HUD's.

Fort Lincoln project sought to serve ends that would be of at least symbolic value to the whole society. Their impulse was to create a community that would be a model for urban society in the second half of the twentieth century. They assumed that different social classes and races could be integrated through a shared attachment to a place and the symbols, lifestyle, and activities associated with it. With an emphasis on "participation" and "decentralization," they also sought to set new styles in social action. And they sought innovation in every aspect of planning, design, and development. In the end, this freight of social significance proved too much for Fort Lincoln to bear. The effort to achieve integration through community yielded a plan of high cost and great complexity. The quest for innovation further inflated objectives and produced a host of economic, technical, and political problems in the final plan.

Why, it may be asked, was the Fort Lincoln project particularly frustrated by the planners' striving for the ideal?

To some extent, the program as a whole was handicapped. The difference between Fort Lincoln and other projects was simply the point at which frustration occurred. In other places, activity stopped before the planning stage. Learning of the program's goals, especially racial and class integration, local officials decided against participating or, having decided to participate, later had to give up in the face of opposition. Fort Lincoln, as the pilot project, had greater momentum, and got far enough along to embody the general objectives in a specific plan.

A second explanation is that, outside of the District of Columbia, HUD proved willing to compromise its objectives for the sake of achieving action. This was what happened in Atlanta. But in the District, Logue was pursuing HUD's objectives with independent commitment, and the high visibility of the project made compromise difficult.

Comparing the Fort Lincoln and Atlanta cases, it is tempting to assert that the closer local adherence was to HUD's objectives, the less likely it was that development would actually occur. However, this proposition ignores the case of Clinton Township, where MDCDA, fully sharing HUD's goals, progressed to the point of construction.

The optimum situation, from HUD's point of view, was that which obtained there. A development agency—a private, nonprofit corporation in this case—had a high degree of autonomy at the local level and shared HUD's goals. In effect, MDCDA was a local "model new communities" agency, committed to technological innovation, provision of housing for the poor, and other leading elements of HUD's guidelines. If such agencies had existed in all local places, and if they had had much authority and scope for action, the prospects for the surplus lands program would have been much better.

Federal Disabilities: the Central Government as Social Activist

In summary, the surplus lands program failed both because the federal government had limited influence at the local level and because it set impossibly high objectives. Its goals exceeded by far its capacity to achieve them.

These causes of failure cannot be dismissed as peculiarities of the program. To be sure, it was peculiar in its impulsive origin and improvised character, but it arose because President Johnson and his aides in the White House believed that other federal programs, especially public housing, were failing. It was designed to make them work better. Very probably, its own failure reveals something about them too.

Fundamentally, the program failed because of characteristics of the federal government that are associated with, and to a degree are inherent in, its central position in the governmental system. These characteristics are the scale of its jurisdiction and its separation from the actual execution of domestic programs. Separation, in turn, results from the division of authority among governments in a federal system and the distance between the "top" and the "bottom" level of government hierarchy in a large, complex society.

These characteristics make it hard for federal policy makers to know what must be done to achieve their objectives locally, and for administrators to bring federal resources, however scarce or plentiful, effectively to bear in local settings. The same characteristics largely account also for the federal tendency to set unrealizeable objectives. The second point, because it is less obvious, requires more elaboration.

Why, in this case, did the idea of a model balanced community find expression in a federal project? Or, why should a federal project begun as an effort to build housing for the poor turn so quickly into an effort to create a model community? The surplus lands program was but one example of a general phenomenon that requires explanation—the tendency of the federal government to be the innovator in American public policy and the source of ideal definitions of the public good.

The division of authority in the federal system has tended to cast the central government in the role of a reformer of local affairs. The fact that the federal government is formally distinct from local governments, yet can be used to influence their conduct, has generated political and administrative activity at the federal level to bring about local change. The federal government is available as an instrument of local reform for interests that wish to use it in that way. It is an especially tempting instrument because it can be used to bring about local change on a wide scale.

Secondly, separation from local politics and administration gives federal policy makers a license to formulate ideal, innovative objectives, because the political and administrative burdens of the innovations they conceive will be borne locally. They are free, much freer than local officials, to stand publicly for progress and high principle. Not having ordinarily to decide concrete cases, they do not have to make the compromises that such cases require. The farther removed they are from the cases, the more principled they are able to be.

Even had the planners of the surplus lands program been more concerned with accommodating to local realities, they would have found this very difficult. The scale and social heterogeneity of the nation, which was the object of their policy making, were so great that they could not possibly take detailed account of the variety of local circumstances that the program might encounter. Guidelines would have to be founded on social theories presumed to be universally applicable and embody values that, from the planners' view at least, were universally desirable.

Having the opportunity to express ideal, progressive objectives, federal policy makers tend to believe that they have the duty. Theirs are the obligations of leadership. And, believing that they have the duty to show other governments what ought to be done, federal officials have developed the strategy of the "demonstration," the single project or program that can be put forth as a model for governmental conduct generally. Though the tangible benefits are restricted to a particular locale, if the project is conceived of as a demonstration the intangible benefits of it can be distributed universally: everyone can share in the symbolic returns from a showing of what the public good requires.

If the federal government did not conceive of its objectives in ideal terms, it could not rely on the demonstration strategy; but the strategy gives further impetus to the striving for the ideal. It might not be possible to build Utopia at Fort Lincoln, but once the federal government became committed to a national demonstration project there, Fort Lincoln's planners could do no less than try. Thus, the strategy of federal conduct as well as the structure of the federal system contributes to the inflation of federal goals.[6]

If the flaws described here are inherent in the federal government, it may be asked why all federal domestic programs do not fail. How do any survive and achieve their purposes? What distinguished the surplus lands program from those that succeed?

One answer is that the degree of federal dependence on local government varies from one domestic function to another. Community development is extremely dependent on local initiative and thus extremely vulnerable to the vicissitudes of local politics.

The peculiar origins of the surplus lands program did handicap it. More than most federal programs, it was centrally conceived. Not only did it originate exclusively at the federal level, but even within the federal government, it received no consideration from the legislature, where local interests are formally represented. Within the ex-

---

6. A full explanation of the federal government's role as reformer and innovator would take account of many other factors, including, for example, its superior revenue-raising capacity, the greater professionalism of its civil service, the activism of its chief executive, and features of its party system. The analysis here emphasizes the one factor that most obviously shapes the federal government's role vis-à-vis local governments—the formal structure of the federal system itself.

ecutive branch, federal officials at the regional level did not participate in the planning of it, nor were local officials invited to do so.
Those officials in the White House and HUD who did plan it did so
in great haste, without themselves making a careful attempt to take
local interests into account.

The usual case is characterized by greater representation of local
interests. The President's proposal may be inspired by the demands of
such interests. In the case of federal aid to education, for example,
although the Johnson Administration in 1965 worked out details of a
feasible program, locally based school organizations had for years
been demanding federal legislation.[7] The typical proposal is submitted to Congress, where local interests again have an opportunity to
make their positions known. And the formulation of administrative
goals or guidelines is likely to follow consultation with local officials.
In these various ways, local interests are more or less systematically
taken into account as the federal government formulates a program.

No doubt, the trend in federal policy making is toward greater cen-
tralization. Increasingly, federal programs are conceived by the President in his search for campaign issues or legislative program material,
and they are planned by his Executive Office or special task forces
and commissions that he has appointed.[8] The surplus lands program
illustrates this trend carried to an extreme.

In the usual case, too, federal programs generate their own local
support by creating organizational allies. When the federal government undertakes a new grant-in-aid program, it specifies that the
local government shall designate an agency to receive funds and
carry out the program. Such agencies tend to become advocates of
the federal purpose at the local level, especially if they are created

7. Frank J. Munger and Richard F. Fenno, Jr., *National Politics and Federal Aid to
Education*, Syracuse University Press, Syracuse, 1962, and Eugene Eidenberg and Roy
D. Morey, *An Act of Congress: The Legislative Process and the Making of Education Pol-
icy*, W. W. Norton and Company, New York, 1969.

8. For example, see Thomas E. Cronin and Sanford D. Greenberg, eds., *The Presidential Advisory System*, Harper Row, New York, 1969. The origins of the anti-
poverty program illustrate the point. See Richard Blumenthal, "The Bureaucracy:
Anti-poverty and The Community Action Program," in Allan P. Sindler, ed., *American Political Institutions and Public Policy*, Little, Brown and Company, Boston, 1969.

anew in response to the federal program and have no other function than to execute it.[9] They also become focal points of activity around which local pressure-group supporters of the federal program can rally. The federal anti-poverty program, for example, although centrally conceived, created its own local support by requiring the formation of community action agencies. More or less by chance, it also "found" a constituency among upwardly mobile blacks whom the civil rights movement had elevated to new heights of political awareness.

Again, the surplus lands program contrasts with the usual case. The federal government took no formal steps to create local allies: it did not require the formation of "model new communities" agencies or agencies for the development of federal surplus lands. Nor was it fortunate enough to find locally a group with enough political awareness and capacity for organization to promote the program.

Federal programs often "work" at the local level—that is, they survive and make progress toward federal goals—because in the usual case an adjustment between the federal program and local interests is worked out. This is an elaborate process, beginning when a federal legislative proposal is formulated and continuing as it gets enacted and administered. Often it is a very time-consuming process. Some federal programs—urban renewal, for example—start very slowly, and pick up momentum only after the original enactment has been amended many times to make it of use to local interests. Years may pass before the program develops a local constituency whose supporting activity will help it to flourish.

No federal programs succeed totally. In the process of adjustment to local interests, purely "federal" purposes are compromised: ideals expressed at the federal level are revised to suit local realities. Yet the adaptation is not on the federal government's part alone. Federal action does influence what happens on the local level, with the net

9. For an analysis of the role of the federal "counterpart" agency, see Martha Derthick, *The Influence of Federal Grants: Public Assistance in Massachusetts*, Harvard University Press, Cambridge, Massachusetts, 1970, pp. 202ff. The case of public assistance in Massachusetts, by contrast with the surplus lands program, illustrates the effectiveness of federal influence at the local level.

result that domestic programs are neither "federal" nor "local," but a blend of the two.

The surplus lands program failed because it was too centralized; it did not incorporate the necessary adjustments to local interests. Perhaps no federal program that seeks to build housing for the poor through the agency of local governments can succeed on a large scale. The federal purpose in this case may be so at odds with the prevailing local interests that no compromise can be worked out that will satisfy the federal purpose very well.[10]

Granting that the surplus lands program suffered from federal disabilities at the local level and from inflated objectives, it might be argued—contrary to the position taken here—that these handicaps are not inherent in federal action. For instance, some might say that the failings were those of the federal chief executive or of a progressive administration. Still others might say that failure occurred not because the program was too centralized, but because it was not centralized enough.

Within the federal government the program was purely presidential, and it suffered from the inability of the President to elicit the necessary support from other elements of the government—Congress and the executive agencies—and then to coordinate them so as to make federal action as effective as possible at the local level. If these other parts of the government had been more responsive to the President's direction (Congress, of course, was not even asked to respond) the program would have had a better chance.

It also suffered from the personality and mode of action of the particular President who started it. Had President Johnson been a more patient and methodical man, the program could have been planned more carefully and would have had a better chance of being founded on workable assumptions. (To be sure, if the President had been a different kind of person, there probably would not have been a program at all.) It seems clear in retrospect that the federal executive agencies initially misled the President as to what they could do, but it

10. The failure of the public housing program should not be exaggerated. Though it has fallen far short of goals, since 1937 it has produced 750,000 units. For recent appraisals of housing programs, see the spring 1970 issue of *The Public Interest*.

is equally clear that the White House invited this error with its demand for instant planning.

Even if the President had been more successful in directing federal action, however, the problems of articulating federal and local action would have remained as a serious handicap. In this case, a distinction between the federal government and the federal chief executive is artificial. He has handicaps of his own within the federal government, but when trying to get something done in the cities he suffers as well, and more fundamentally, from the handicaps of the government he leads.

As an effort to house the poor and, even more, as an effort to build model communities, the program was more likely to have come from a liberal than a conservative administration. It is arguable that at least one of the disabilities it revealed—the tendency to set ideal, innovative objectives—is characteristic not of federal administrations generally, but only of those that are "progressive." Crudely put, the failure of the surplus lands program was of a kind that could happen only to the Democrats. Other kinds of failure, those that come from doing too little rather than trying to do too much, presumably afflict the Republicans.

The history of the program does not have very much to say on this point, since it deals almost entirely with a Democratic administration, but what it does say suggests that the differences between federal administrations are differences of degree rather than kind. The Nixon Administration, despite its many reservations, did not repudiate Fort Lincoln. Although this was a hastily conceived personal project of a President of the opposite party and although the goals stated for it were of very doubtful feasibility, the Nixon Administration did not say that it would abandon them. Moreover, that it failed fully to commit itself to Fort Lincoln is in part to be accounted for by the fact that it was engaged in a more or less analogous undertaking of its own. Rebuilding the riot areas in Washington, if less "innovative" or "idealistic" than building a model new community, was equally an expression of the federal propensity to undertake symbolic demonstrations in local affairs.[11]

11. The Nixon Administration did find a politically feasible, even profitable, use

If the federal government is to achieve its domestic aims, perhaps it should pursue them independently, without relying on local governments. If it had centralized the surplus lands program altogether and tried to develop the land itself, it might have accomplished more. Given the present state of constitutional law, there would have been no constitutional barrier to its doing so. There are several reasons why the President and HUD did not take this approach.

The federal government would have had to start afresh as an administrator of community development. The President would have had to ask new authority and appropriations from Congress, and he would have had to enlarge HUD very much or create a new federal administrative agency. Local agencies for community development were already organized, and it seemed faster and cheaper to rely on them than to contrive a means of direct federal action. At least in Washington, where the program was formed, the local redevelopment agency was eager to take the initiative. In summary, direct federal action, even in the national capital, would have been a major departure from the usual way of carrying out community development, requiring a radical revision of custom and existing arrangements.

Relying on local agencies seemed so much the natural thing to do that the federal administration did not make a serious effort to do otherwise. It did consider a compromise form of direct action—bypassing the local government to deal with a private developer—but no such arrangement was concluded. In Clinton Township, MDCDA was technically an agent of the local government. Though HUD's surplus lands project office sought to carry out development in San Antonio without support from the local government, it soon gave up. Within HUD it had encountered resistance from the budget office, which rightly saw the effort as a major departure from existing policy and practice in intergovernmental relations.

---

for surplus land. Early in 1970 it launched the Legacy of Parks program, intended to transfer federal land to state and local governments for recreation. As of the fall of 1971, fifty-seven tracts totalling 15,400 acres and worth nearly $70 million had been or were about to be conveyed (*Wall Street Journal*, September 13, 1971, p. 32). According to the *Journal*, President Nixon got the idea for the program while strolling along a federally owned beach near the Western White House at San Clemente.

Even if direct federal action were practicable, it might not be effective. Obstacles to achievement of federal goals are internal to the federal government as well as external; and if the federal administration grew much bigger and more complex, problems of coordination and control *within* the federal government—which are serious already—would be increased manyfold. Beyond this, as the federal government supplanted local governments in the performance of domestic functions, it would have to assume the political burdens that they now bear and that are often the principal obstacle to accomplishment. Citizen demands that now are addressed to local governments would be addressed to it.[12] If it responded, it would be no more able to act on controversial matters than local governments are. If it did not respond, democracy would be ill served.

Presently the federal government shares most domestic functions with local governments, and in respect to financing and administration, there is an obvious logic to the sharing. The federal government, better able to raise revenue than local governments, helps them with financial aid. Local governments, better organized collectively to execute programs, help the federal government with administration. The "logic," if any, of the sharing of political functions in the federal system is more obscure, but such a logic may exist.

In shared programs, both the federal government and local governments have a political function: both play a part in defining the objectives of public action and in responding to differences of value, interest, and opinion. The federal government, being removed from particular and parochial conflicts, is better able to express idealistic and progressive objectives. Local governments, more deeply engaged in these conflicts, are better able to respond to the actual preferences of active political interests.

In this system, the accomplishments of government constantly fall short of the objectives expressed at the federal level, and disillusionment follows among both the public and public officials. Such a sys-

---

12. As the Nixon Administration was aware. It considered direct federal action for development of Fort Lincoln, but as one memorandum noted, "HUD would be put in the position of dealing directly with Fort Lincoln citizen participation groups, a precedent which may not be wise."

tem may nevertheless be fairly well adapted to the governing of a very large and diverse society—providing, as it does, for the expression both of abstract ideals and of particular, tangible interests. In the process of governing, the two have to be reconciled. Tension between the federal and local governments in the American system may be one sign that such reconciliation is occurring.

GLOSSARY OF ACRONYMS

CAP — Community Action Program, coordinator locally of the antipoverty programs of the Office of Economic Opportunity

FELCUN — Federal Lands for Critical Urban Needs*

FHA — Federal Housing Administration, a division of HUD

GSA — General Services Administration of the federal government

HUD — Department of Housing and Urban Development

MDCDA — Metropolitan Detroit Citizens Development Authority

NCPC — National Capital Planning Commission, of the District of Columbia

NDP — Neighborhood Development Program, a local activity supported by HUD's urban renewal program

NTIT — New Towns In-Town*

RAA — Renewal Assistance Administration of HUD (no longer so designated)

RLA — Redevelopment Land Agency, the District of Columbia urban renewal agency

SLCD — Surplus Lands for Community Development*

* All of these, FELCUN, NTIT, and SLCD, are different terms for the same new towns in-town program.